Unlocking Your Abundance with Mary Magdalene

Manifesting with the Power of Roses

Kim Ora Rose

White Flame Publishing

ISBN-13: 9798352310199
ISBN-10:

White Flame Publishing
Burton on Trent
Staffordshire
United Kingdom
www.orarosetemple.com
Cover design by: Natasha Murray
Library of Congress Control Number: 2018675309
Printed in the United Kingdom

This book is dedicated to my husband Philip and my dearest friends Margaret Hunt and Ishtara Rose who have both inspired me to create this book.

Also to all my family and those that have been part of my Rose Temple group.

Unlocking Your Abundance Journal

Manifesting with the Power of Roses - Journal

You might like to buy the 22 Days Journal to accompany this course it is designed with pages for each day for you to record your experiences. It is available on www.orarosetemple.com or Amazon

Paperback Internationally

https://www.amazon.co.uk/dp/BOBCRXJN2F

Today
Awaken to your unity
Listen to your soul
Sit in silence and hear your inner voice
Let the negative thoughts go
Let go of self restrictions
Be at one with your inner heart
Feel the love open from your heart centre
Like the rose flower bud opening into a bloom
Feel the love expand into your whole being
Out into your aura and into your energy fields
See more rose buds expanding, opening up to infinity love
Love is the only language of Love
Love is the language of creation
Be part of Mother's Earth's creation
Be a bloom in your life
Be connected to everything
The new earth is yours
KIM ORA ROSE

Contents

Introduction

On midsummer's day in 2019 I visited Sainte Baume Grotte the cave of Mary Magdalene in Provence, South of France and when I came out I was changed.

Within the cave I received the most beautiful light of peace, love and happiness. I call this Pink Bliss Light of Mary Magdalene and it embedded within this 22 day course of manifesting abundance with eight roses.

This course will unlock abundance in your life, bringing joy, happiness and pure love. As you connect each day with Mary Magdalene's energies to help you to fully unlock ultimate abundance, joy and happiness. It is a process of deeply connecting to your wants and needs to fully appreciate all you already have in your life and open internal doors to receive more abundance, love and happiness. With this 22 days course with daily intentions and meditations which can be downloaded as MP3s you will follow a program of listening to each of the meditations, they are quite short but very powerful. You will go on an inner journey with Mary Magdalene's wisdom and her transformational power of eight roses.

Roses are very powerful flowers associated with Mary Magdalene and Mother Mary.

As you connect with each of your energy centres you will create opportunities for your fullest potential for peace, love, happiness, creativity and joy. With each day of the course you will dissolve your internal blockages to be fully open to unlimited abundance with the loving support of Mary Magdalene and Mother Mary. The 22 days course is a program of meditations following the seven chakras of the body with a corresponding rose ray. As you listen to each of the rose meditations for each day of the week for 22 days you will release your blockages to fullness of joy and abundance to move from 3D conditioning to 5D realisation.

You can follow the meditations and intentions for 8 days or 8 weeks or the full 22 days the choice is yours. You will open yourself up to receive abundance from whichever way you follow the course. The deepest transformation with come from the full 22 days, but if you don't have that commitment or time you dive in with daily meditations for eight days or over eight weeks.

Each time you reconnect with each Chakra, Rose Rays and Divine Guidance of Mary Magdalene to dissolve your blockages to feeling full abundance, health, joy, happiness and wellbeing. Blockages and resistance to change will melt away to bring you to the fullness of abundance in every aspect of your life. In return your gratitude and connection to the deep love of Mary Magdalene and Mother Mary will fill your well, fill your chalice, fill your ever flowing creativity and joy.

Abundance means "a very large quantity of something" it also means the idea of having plenty in expressions of fullness, joy, strength of mind, body and soul in spiritual perspective. In this book the program is concerned with achieving unlimited abundance from the pursuit of releasing blockages to plentiful materials and internal resistances to receiving and acknowledging prosperity. Initially this course was created to release these internal, material and spiritual blockages by changing the mind, body and soul's perceptions by removing old emotions, patterns and conditionings that hold someone back in all aspects. The course was created with daily practice of connecting with each of the body's energy centres, with the seven traditional chakras and the corresponding colours.

Chakras are circular vortexes of energy that are place in seven different points on the spinal column. All of the chakras are connected to the different organs and glands within the body. Chakras are in charge of distributing life force energy around the body, this is called Chi, Qi or Praana.

If a chakra is blocked or unbalanced, the life force energy becomes blocked and this can affect mental or wellbeing ailments. When all the seven chakras are in balance they bring harmony to physical wellbeing, emotional and mental states of mind.

The seven chakras and their colours are:

Sahasrara- Crown Chakra - White or Purple

Ajna - 3rd Eye Chakra - Indigo

Vishuddha - Throat Chakra - Blue

Anahata - Heart Chakra - Green or Pink

Manipura -Solar Plexus Chakra - Yellow

Swadhithana - Sacral Chakra - Orange

Muladhara - Root Chakra - Red

Plus

Higher Heart - Thymus Chakra - Soft Pink Bliss

Mary Magdalene brings her essence to the higher heart chakra, this light is within this course, it is in the Pink Bliss Meditation, the first energy of Abundance of self, I now offer attunements to this energy and you can find out about this on my website www.orarosetemple.com

This Higher Heart Chakra is at the centre of these teachings it brings balance to all the chakras and lights up the body to receive more and more light from the Soul Star Chakra and Stella Gateway Chakra, if the higher heart is open wide you can receive many blessings from all that is, including light language, light codes, Starseed awakenings, ascension and so much more.

As part of this course there is an eight chakra the higher heart that is associated with the colour pink and this is the chakra connected to the Pink Bliss energies of the first meditation. This chakra is the etheric heart it is sometimes called the thymus chakra or high heart chakra. It is associated with divine love, compassion and connects to the language of the heart.

It is an area for forgiveness and seeking truth and a place of heart expansion and light language. This chakra is situated above your heart and below your throat chakra, it is one of the glands that develop whilst the fetus is in the womb. This gland is connected to the immune system which is interesting as the ascension and awakening of the planet leads us to open our higher heart chakra wider by connecting to our search for divine love, spiritual love and as we are going through this enormous awakening our immune system is so important.

We hold our DNA coding and other key information in the Higher Heart chakra together with the ways we communicate with others. The language of our heart comes from the Higher Heart, my poems and channelling come more and more from higher heart and as you connect with the Pink Bliss energies your higher heart will expand more and more. Very powerful healing comes from this chakra from many places within your emotional and physical bodies as you invite in the deepest love.

The higher heart chakra oversees the immune system and when it is open and balanced it can help ward off infections like the flu, colds, covid and it helps throat infections too. It has a lovely vibration that brings comfort and peace, it helps to balance the upper chakras from the lower ones to the heart and higher chakras. It has a calming effect on the body and mind and you will notice this straight away when you listen to the Pink Bliss meditation and read the intentions.

After working with chakras for healing, meditation and development for several years a process was formed to use the colours and energy centres together with intentions/meditation to balance each of the chakras. This course was created with rose meditations as a focus with each chakra and its colour to unblock old patterning of thinking. The course was facilitated with a group in a private facebook group in the summer of 2019 and has been updated with new meditations and this accompanying book.

The meditations are now MP3 instead of short videos for better access to them. The course remains 22 days long with the a structured program following the introductory first day with Pink Bliss meditation and the seven chakras over 21 weeks. Mary Magdalene was a healer and she is channelled into the meditations with her subtle messages of love and peace.

The program has been created from several years of healing practice and the authors own healing journey of releasing, unblocking and letting go of old emotions to be fully free with unlimited abundance. At times in her own life she sought abundance through a teaching career but was overworked, over tried and found more joy and happiness through letting go of old conditioning.

It begins with you
Are you Ready?
Abundance is your true essence
Happiness, Joy
& Pure Love is Waiting for you

22 Days Course Structure

This course will unlock your abundance, joy, health, wealth, happiness and pure love in your life. It has been developed with my teachings and channeled meditation with Mary Magdalene and Mother Mary.

I hope you enjoy the experience. The meditations are short but very powerful so you can listen to them daily during the 22 days. You can download the eight Meditations from my website   please visit my website, contact us and we will send you details of how to download the free meditations.

If you are a healer you may use self healing as part of the daily exercises eg you may wish to channel self healing whilst listening to the meditations. Every day you can listen to one of the eight meditations either by reading in the book or by listening to one of the free mp3 audios; there are seven core meditations pertaining to each of the chakras plus Pink Bliss meditation with the pink rose of self love.

(You can download the link is at the back of the book.) The meditations are short so you can fit them into your life, you will receive eight meditations in the form of MP3s they are available for download on my website.

Day One - Mary Magdalene Pink Bliss - Pink Rose
Step One - Root Chakra - Ruby Rose
Step Two - Sacral Chakra - Orange Rose
Step Three - Solar Plexus - Yellow Rose
Step Four - Heart Chakra - Red Rose
Step Five - Throat Chakra - Blue Rose
Step Six - 3rd Eye Chakra - Indigo Rose
Step Seven - Crown Chakra - White Rose

This is a journey into abundance and of ascension for as we tune into our inner selves we connect to our old programming and conditioning to release these thought patterns. Transformation begins to takes place with the healing power of each rose linking to the different aspects of our thoughts connecting to our energy centres eg the root chakra holds emotions pertaining to money and security.

During this course you will connect to each chakra in turn for each of the three weeks and as you do so you will fully embrace the fullness of abundance and will notice shifts within your old programming as this is transformed with the loving energy of Mary Magdalene, the rose energies of the Way of Love and more limitless opportunities will flow to you.

This is a journey of healing and transformation its something you may wish do once or once a year. For we always clearing old patterns to step fully into the fullness of our own abundance as we dissolve old patterns in our lives. Moving from suffering and lack thoughts/ belief systems that you can not have abundance, joy and happiness in your life into unlimited possibilities for your own unlimited abundance, happiness and joy. People do not have to continue through cycles of suffering, you might recognise in yourself how you go round and round in suffering. This course shows you the ways to fully express yourself and your emotions so you can move your expressions into feeling gratitude. The course helps you remove barriers and your inner resistance to changes that will bring powerful changes to your daily life.

In the past you may have been searching for your purpose or your unique gifts, with the focus of getting somewhere, this doesn't always lead to the joy that we seek. This is journey of going within, feeling everything and releasing it; feeling the fullness of abundance and being it. The old masculine way of "getting" things, of acquiring things e.g. cars, homes, etc. This is now dissolving, structures are changing the new earth, paradigm is coming in each and every day. This is the way of the feminine and you will be fully supported by the Divine Feminine of Mary Magdalene throughout this course.

I often refer to the *Way of Love* this is sometimes called the Way of the Rose, these are the teachings of Mary Magdalene and Jesus. This course will open your heart more to the the *Way of Love,* as you connect each day with the meditations. You will uncover more and more of your own wisdom and connection to Mary Magdalene. As you journey through each of the Seven Steps you will move more into a sense of balance within yourself; of finding your *true self* to gratitude for all that you already have. Gratitude is one of the simplest ways to develop abundance learning how to be grateful for everything in your life is one of the most important lessons in life.

When you give thanks for the things in your life e.g. for your home, family etc you begin to realise that you have so much. This changes your desires in the form of wants and needs as you become fully aware of how much you really do have. As you fully embrace a position of gratitude you will receive signs from the universe to guide you on your life's path, believe in miracles for they do happen each and every day.

At times and especially this year during the pandemic some of the old conditioning has been coming up again for me, with the fears of health, fear of other people's health and wellbeing and general anxiety about the Covid situation.

In these times I sometimes have to vent what I'm feeling, fully feeling it and then go into the peace; the bliss energy I share that with you in the first MP3 meditation when you meet the Pink Bliss energy. So when you feel any emotions that come up you can feel them fully, acknowledge them then move into a place of peace. This is much healthier than trying to bury them or ignore them as doing this leads to holding the emotion much longer than you need to and can build up resentment.

So when old conditioning 3D energy comes up e.g fear about the virus, worrying about the "lockdowns", angry about situations you can not control, sit with it allow it to be expressed, then return to balance with the peace energy of pure love. You will quickly learn how to step into the peace energy of bliss, it is a bit like the energy, vibration of being in the *now* but with the added energy of

Mary Magdalene fully supporting you.

Going into the vibration of gratitude for everything you have in your life changes your whole vibration in to one of abundance.

These are some of the core elements of the universal laws for attracting and being fully in gratitude and peace. When you feel rich with unlimited abundance of everything your whole attitude, sense of being, vibrational frequency shifts and opens you up to more and more abundance. During times of slipping into the old programming of fear, doubts etc I have had to really focus on being back in the light energy with gratitude.

This really works for me and I am sure it will for you too. If you stay too long in the attitude of not having this brings more of the same "not having" experiences and again this is universal law of attraction, if you are in the energy of lack, not having, you attract that energy.

You will experienced times of being in flow and when you are spending more of your time with thoughts and feelings of abundance you will experience more and more flow. Again this is law of attraction energies of being in flow, brings more flow, being in the energy of peace and balance brings more joy and happiness and being in gratitude brings more abundance.

So is something comes up allow yourself some time to fully feel it, then give yourself some time to really connect to the pink bliss energy and gratitude for everything you have and see how this affects your emotions, thoughts, ways of being as you learn to be more and more in the energy of the Way of Love. This is the energy vibration, of being in loving life, loving yourself, loving others and unconditional love.

The way you interpret life's experiences has alot to do with how you feel about yourself, if you love yourself and acknowledge the fact you can have unlimited abundance in your life you will attract good experiences. Abundance of health has been a key theme this year and finding the way to live a happy healthy life is at the fore front of most of our thoughts, how to improve our immune system and our thoughts are so linked to our health. When we are stressed or holding on to negative thoughts and emotions they can affect our health.

So to free yourself to attract an abundance of health in your life you need to raise your vibration.

During these ascension times of moving forward everything is being speeded up to do the powerful shifts in heart chakra and love vibration that is flowing all around our planet and dimensions. When this love vibration comes into contact with denser emotions of rage, fear, sadness and anger it can get stored in our bodies and energy fields and our bodies react with a natural cleansing process, we may get a cold or have other ways for our bodies to cleanse our emotions.

There are lots of many effective ways of clearing old emotions and transforming them into new opportunities and new high vibrational frequencies. Within the meditations you will feel each blockage, emotion and then feel the peace and gratitude and this is an energetic way of transforming old energies into something new that is one of peace, balance, joy and happiness. You may feel what we call *shifts*, they are coming in this year, day after day, you will feel a shifts of energy our earth is healing, changing its vibration, creating the new earth, it is all part of the ascension process.

Sometimes it can take a few days to receive each shift and they can be unsettling especially at the time of a new moon or full moon phase. Therefore I would recommend you listening to the Bliss meditation to assist with these energy shifts. It will transport you to a place of peace and balance.

In the program this is the first meditation you may listen to it throughout the course as you feel guided to, each time you will connect to Mary Magdalene and receive her guiding light. This energy is soft pink very peaceful and loving. In just 20 mins a day you can really make some changes in your life with these meditations to guide and Mary Magdalene to support as you fully feel each chakra's energies and fully embrace peace, bliss and gratitude. You may wish to listen to the meditations once or twice a day and add reiki or other healing modalities to your daily exercises to fully enhance your experiences.

You could channel self healing energies whilst you listen to the meditation or set an intention to receive healing whilst you are listening to the meditations. I teach several different Reiki healing modalities including Rose Reiki and Infinite if you are interested please visit my website to find out more about these courses. www.orarosetemple.com

Sweet Dreams

Aims & Objectives

Aims

Manifesting Abundance

Learn to fully live in the *Way of Love*

Receive joyfulness and happiness

Receive abundance of love, health, wealth and creation

Objectives

Connect with the magical power of roses

Connect deeply with Mary Magdalene's wisdom

Connect with your sacred gifts

Connect to infinite love & joy

Experience daily teachings to dissolve lack in your life

Find the Gratitude for all you have

Unlocking Your Chakras

There are eight chakras that we focus on in this book and these run from the base of the spine to the crown of the head, each has it's own meaning and colour associated with it.

There are seven main chakras that most people focus on and in this book there is a focus on the 8th chakra associated with the Higher Heart. The colours are follow the same colours of the rainbow. This chakra system began in India between 1500 and 500 BC and is in the oldest texts called Vedas. In the body there are one hundred of chakras in addition to these main seven, there are chakras in the hands and feet and many more but we tend to focus on these seven. What is a chakra? The word means a spinning disk or wheel, it relates to a wheel of energy that runs along the spine. The health of a person's chakra is connected to the well being of the body, mind and emotional well being of a person.

The colours of each chakra hold a vibration and frequency and these colours are well known. We respond to colours and these help us to understand the chakras and how they respond to our energy. Many people enjoy connecting to the colours and in this book you will be doing this when you connect to each rose that corresponds to each chakra. The first step is to connect to your Higher Heart an 8th Chakra between your Heart and Throat this is about self love and the Pink Bliss of Mary Magdalene is associated with Self Love. Archangel Chamuel is also associated with this Higher Heart Chakra.

Each of the chakras are energy centres and as you learn more about them and the associated colours and frequencies you will understand how they affect your abundance and happiness. The eight chakras in your body start at your spine and go up your body to your crown at the top of your head. They vibrate and help you live your live. Energy can not be created or destroyed and the energy that flows through your body and chakras is "Chi" or "universal energy" this energy is always flowing around your body and as it does so you are affected by its flow. At times different chakras can get blocked or stuck and this affects the human body and mind. It can affect your energy levels, your mood swings and feelings and over time can cause illnesses.

As you follow this course you will be releasing energy blockages in each of the chakras to allow a natural flow of energy to flow throughout your entire body. This will bring you harmony and joy. There are different ways you can balance your chakras including: Chakra Balancing with energy healing e.g reiki or with crystals, through meditation, exercise e.g yoga, qi gong or tai chi, through the use of colour or music.

In this course you will be using colour, meditation and flower energies from the roses together with the energies of Mary Magdalene and other spiritual guides. You may wish to use crystals too to add to your daily meditations, either by placing them in the room where you meditate, carry one in your pocket or hold one when you meditate.

These are some suggestions for crystals to use to correspond to each step.

Higher Heart
Pink Rose Quartz
Root   Red
Bloodstone, Obsidian, Jet, Garnet
Sacral Orange
Carnelian, Amber, Orange Calcite
Solar Plexus
Yellow Citrine, Yellow Topaz, Tigers Eye
Heart
Green or Pink Green Aventurine, Emerald, Peridot
Throat
Blue   Blue Lace Agate, Angelite, Aquamarine
Third Eye
Indigo Lapis Lazuli, Sodalite, Azurite
Crown
White or Purple   Clear Quartz, Apophyllite, Amethyst

In addition to crystals there are metals that associate with each of the chakras these are:

Higher Heart and Heart - Platinum
Root - Lead
Sacral - Copper
Solar Plexus - Gold
Throat - Mercury
Third Eye - Silver

Crown - Gold

You may choose to wear a pendant or other jewellery with one of the crystals when you are following the program eg if you are aiming to open up your crown chakra more you may wear a gold an amethyst ring or pendant. Or if you wish to let go of fear and worries about money you may chose lead or pewter with garnets.

These are just suggestions, you could set an altar up for this course to set your intentions as a ritual. Where you place crystals, metals, flowers, candles etc to represent the elements.

Sacred Space

When you start this course you may wish to set up a sacred space for the program, it may be in the space you will listen to the meditations, write in your journal or read this book. This is a very powerful way of starting the course and setting powerful intentions for your outcomes from this course. You can do this in a ceremony or ritual and its will have a profound affect on your outcomes as you follow this course.

The aim is to create a space to honour Mary Magdalene and Mother Mary and you can do this by creating an Altar. It does not have to be very big, it can be on a shelf, stand, small corner of the room etc. I used my windowsill by my computer as it is near me when I am writing or recording my meditations. It is up to you where you place yours. It can be in your home or you may like to set up a crystal grid or altar in your garden, I often set up a crystal grid in my garden and have a sacred space under my arch.

I call this my temple but it is up to you whether you choose to set up sacred space or not and how you do it.

These are some suggestions:

Create a sacred space with something to represent each

of the chakras, something of each colour, this could be different colour crystals, you can buy chakra crystal sets quite easily on the internet.

Create a space to honour your spiritual guides on this program, Mary Magdalene and Mother Mary. Include the elements of Fire, Air, Water, Earth and Spirit.

Fire - Set up candles can use different colours of the chakras or white

Air – Incense or add feathers

Water – Chalice or glass of water, you may wish to add sacred water from a local well or springs.

Earth – Salt or crystals, you may use what you already have or select ones to represent the chakras.

Flowers – Roses in pink, red, white or any other colour that feels right to you. You could add other flowers too. Just add what feels right.

Metals - Copper, tin, gold or silver adding metals to represent the chakras.

Special objects - statue or Altar cards eg images of Mary Magdalene or other deities.

Use your intuition of what feels right I suggest you set up your sacred space when you start the course and you can change it each week by adding fresh flowers, changing the water and cleansing the crystals etc.

When you set up your sacred space you can say an intention or prayer over the space.

Do what ever feels right for you.

Power of the Moon

The different moon phases can assist with this course, preferably you might commence the course on a Full Moon or a New Moon as each of these have powerful energies that can affect your journey through the 22 days.

The moon phases move through different phases throughout the month from a new moon through to the full moon. The moon is very mystical and in ancient times there were many myths about it. You will have no doubt heard about how the full moon affects people. If you are spiritual the moon phases might be part of your life, it is associated with the Triple Goddess and with the Wheel of Life. There are three phases of the goddess that relate to maiden, mother and crone and these are phases within a year. The Triple Goddess is the moon phases and the Sun is the God. These phases represent the life cycle of birth, life and death and rebirth.

The moon has a power over us on earth and you will notice now you feel when there is a full moon. The moon also affects our tides around the world you may have read about how the full moon can affect the spring tides.

It is the gravitational pull that affects the tides and

because we are made up of 80% water the moon affects us too. There are four distinct phases to the lunar cycle these are the new moon, waxing moon, full moon and waning moon. The lunar cycle starts with the new moon, the skies are dark as you can not see the moon at this phase and it moves each night to become the waxing moon, through to the full moon, then to the waning moon and back to a new moon.

The New Moon has so much potential even though it can't be see, it is the start of the lunar cycle. This occurs every 28 days. The new moon is a time to start things, for new beginnings a time to make plans and set intentions. Perfect time to start this 22 days program as it gives you the energy of new beginnings.

The Waxing Moon starts to appear as a crescent in the night's sky, as the power starts to build up to the full moon, this cycle takes 14 days. The waxing moon is a good time to start working on your self confidence, self worth etc.

The Full Moon is very powerful and it can be used to help manifest our desires and our blockages. It is a great time for rituals and ceremonies and for charging up the power in your crystals. You can place them under the full moon to charge them up. Just as you can charge up your crystals, you can stand under the full moon and draw down the moons energy too.

The Waning Moon begins after the full moon as the power wanes as it moves toward a new moon again. This can be a time of reflection, reviewing and letting go, a good time for releasing and cleansing old patterns and thoughts.

Therefore each of the moon phases are important and you might like to harness the power of a New Moon or Full Moon when you start this course.

Power of Roses

Roses have been recognised throughout time as a sacred symbol of purity, peace and love. The pink rose is deeply connected to Mary Magdalene and it holds the purist energies of self love, of self worth and bliss. Roses are a flower of great beauty, they express promise, hope, new beginnings and contrasted by the thorns symbolising defence and loss.

Roses have been loved for centuries and been used as symbols throughout different cultures, religions, organisations and art. They represent Love, Honour, Faith, Beauty, Balance, Passion, Wisdom, Intrigue, Devotion, Sensuality and Timelessness. You many have already worked energetically with the Pink Rose of Mary Magdalene or of Mother Mary of self love.

In the Freemasonry, there are three roses which symbolise the guiding principles of Love, Life and Light. Also in Christianity the rose bush is said to have grown out of the site of Christ's death. His blood serving is offering associated with a red rose and the thorns symbolised as the ultimate sacrifice.

There are several roses in the Tarot Cards, where the Rose is a symbol of balance. The beauty of the rose expresses promise, new beginnings and hope contrasting again with the thorns of defence, physicality, loss and thoughtlessness. The Rose is seen on the Magician, Strength, Death and Fool cards all which hold strong meanings of balance and equilibrium.

The Magdalene Rose is usually symbolised as a Pink Rose for self love and deep connection to Mary for her beauty, passion, compassion, healing skills and her love. Pink Roses have been dated as far back as 40 million years. In China's Imperial rose garden about 5,000 years ago they grew pink roses and have continued to be grown in history every since. Pink Roses are the classic colour of roses; they were the first rose cultivated as they are the most common colour to go in the wild.

During the Victorian times the pink rose was used to decorate greetings card, wallpaper etc. Many of the Goddesses are connected to the rose symbolism and with our ideas of love and beauty such as with Inanna, Ishtar, Aphrodite, Venus, Isis and Magdalene.

As you connect deeply with each of the rose colours you will become more connected to the universe, source energies, Mary Magdalene.

In this course I have used the power of eight different coloured roses to associate with the seven chakra energy centres and added a pink rose to symbolise Mary Magdalene's pink bliss energy. I am a colour therapy healer and use different colours to direct healing to different parts of the body.

This is a very powerful way of using colour to direct healing to different areas with the chakra energy systems. In the past I was creating a healing system of identifying energy blockages, unbalanced chakra symptoms and healing this imbalance you can do this in a single session.

Over time the chakras can become unbalanced again and this was something that Dr Usui also found when healing the people with reiki healing. That even though the reiki healing, crystal healing, chakra balancing, spiritual healing all bring balance. In time the client will require further healing because the old patterning, conditioning remains.

Therefore there is a requirement to look beyond the "quick fix" of energy healing to balance your chakras and go deeper into each emotion and 3 dimensional patterning as we move towards the New Earth.

As a healer I often use the main energy centres as a focus of intention, I learnt about the main seven chakras of the body when learning about healing in the early 2000s and the other chakras that direct energy around the body. When I was facilitating Angel meditation groups I started working with a 13 chakra system for meditation connections and healing. You can read about this system on my website. This was developed with inner guidance from my higher self and angels.

Several years ago I started creating a deeper way of unlocking past emotions with each chakra to allow old emotions to be released and new patterns to form. I have discovered that with a combination of healing words in the meditations and the connection to different colours that a client can release old emotions and energy blockages so that they can open themselves up to unlimited abundance. The process becomes even more powerful with the added energies of the Divine Feminine of Mary Magdalene. I have used these techniques in person with clients and seen some remarkable transformation.

I wanted to share these techniques with more people so I launched the first course with people in a private online group and now offer the updated course materials and mp3 audios.

The Way of Love

This is the way to live in love, the way to love yourself deeply and always honour yourself, the way of love is the Way of the Rose, it is the core of the teachings of Mary Magdalene and Yeshua.

The Way of Love is embedded within all of my meditations, its is the returning to yourself, to fully accept and understand yourself and it brings you home to yourself. As you truly "dive in" to "know yourself" you begin a healing process of transformation to step into yourself.

Core teachings from Mary Magdalene are to love yourself, release your old patterns, let go of feelings of not having everything you wish for and knowing that you are a beautiful Soul.

I am writing a book with Jesus and Mary Magdalene about the Way of Love and this will be published later in 2022.

One step at a time
One day at a time
Releasing
Remembering who you truly are

In gratitude
Of all you have
And, all you are
With love
That is the Way of Love

by Kim Ora Rose

Mary Magdalene

Mary, Sophia. Miriam

Mary Magdalene was a real human being, who existed in history, as, indeed, did Jesus. Gods and Goddesses, as a rule, have always lived in heaven, never on earth. She is often said to have been a reincarnation of Isis the Eternal Goddess. She is an ascended master who returns to us to rise up and rejoice as we reunite with the femininity of ourselves, within each of us there is a union of male and female, Jesus and Mary are that perfect union of balance male and female.

In history Mary is remembered but not for her part she was a healer, a scholar and compassionate discipline. You may have read the Gospel of Mary that was found in the Dead Sea Scrolls in 1946 these help us to know Mary Magdalene more through her own Gospel. Yet it is through our direct channelling with her essence that we truly come to know her.

I have been channelling with Mary Magdalene since 2015 and maybe before for she has been a constant guide. I have had several visions of a life with her and Yeshua in dreams and past life regresssion. She comes to me as a friend, spiritual teacher and way shower, she brings her messages of hope, peace and her way of love. This is at the heart of everything I write about and in my day to day life.

I believe Mary Magdalene to have landed at Sainte Maries de la Mer with the other Maries to begin a life in the South of France, there are many places with stories of her performing baptisms at Carasonne, living and worshiping at Sainte Baume, Provence, connections to Rennes le Chateaux and many more.

I have visited some of these places and felt her deepest love and connection there. "Within a past life I lived at the time of Magdalene within the families connected to the Essenes my life was planned to be of service to the coming Messiah to that of Yeshua and his beloved, this was Mary Magda, she was my spiritual teacher and companion, my family chose me me to be betrothed to Michael when I was reaching womanhood, before this they sent me away to learn all the ways of the great ancient Mysteries so that I could be a healer for my community.

There were too many intrusions to the life that was planned for Yeshua and Mary for they were destined for great teachings.

They were bringing *"The Way"* and new *"Way"* with religion, taking back the scriptures to their "Core Way" this was the *"Way of Love"*. Their love for one another was of mutual respect and of perfect balance but this was not be on their earthly plane and this was taken from them far to soon. The rising of the conflicts that were against

Yeshua's teaching grew far and wide as the heads of state, heads of religious houses feared the changes of though and resisted a new "*Way of Being*" so the crucifixion came much sooner than the Elders in the Essenes expected and all was changed so quickly. " I am bringing "The Way of Love" in my courses and spiritual teaching, the power of roses in this course and meditation.

If Mary Magdalene calls to you to join her with her teachings' bringing the mystical ways of ancient times into your modern lives. You may have been receiving signs for Mary Magdalene, seeing more Roses, feathers, if you have been on a spiritual path for some time it may be the right time to dive into yourself, a year of self learning and remembering and reconnecting to the Divine Feminine. You may have heard the call from the Divine Feminine if you are reading these words.

In June 2019 I went with my husband on a Pilgrimage to the South of France we visited several places on our holiday including Sainte Maximum's Bascilla where the skull of Mary Magdalene is kept in the crypt and Sainte Baume the Mary Magdalene cave near Nans le Pins, Var, Provence. We visited the cave on Midsummer's day 21st June 2019.

The journey to the Mary Magdalene cave was quite arduous for me as I have asthma; it was a hot day so we chose to start the journey early in the morning. Most of the pathway was covered in trees until we reached the rocky cliff, the terrain was constantly ascending up the mountain, following winding paths, we paused so many times. Whilst I was determined to reach the cave I did at times wonder if I would actually make it to the cave. I was really struggling with my breathing top, with the heat, the incline and my own breathing disabilities.

We met people coming down who were struggling in the opposite direction. My husband was very patient and encouraging with me, at times I could only take around 20 steps then have to rest, take some water and my inhaler then start again.

We enjoyed all of the pauses listening to the bells ringing out from Sainte Baume Hostellerie urging us to continue and thus we did, pausing to listen to the birds singing and the sound of water flowing down the mountain.

The woodland is full of oak trees and these sacred trees don't often grow in this area of France, they are full of ancient knowledge and wisdom and the oak leaf and acorn are long associated with Magdalene.

Eventually we arrived at the steps to the cave and walked past the roses with the statues of Jesus on the Cross and Mary Magdalene around the gardens. We looked out over the landscape over the mountainous terrain and down to the flatter landscape. When we went into the cave out of respect I covered my head and arms with a soft cream scarf, a gift from a friend. This was a perfect gift with tiny butterflies adorning it and it was light and easy to carry, it felt so precious to wear to cover my head and shoulders.

There were roses everywhere in small vases and candles to light, by the statue on the lower level I remember recording some orbs as I sat and looked around. When

I fell into beautiful Bliss energy, just a wave of loving energy washed over me and I felt a presence on my shoulder, like a whisper, I felt held, in love, it was most amazing feeling of being held by love, in peace, in calm, in bliss. This is the only way I can describe it, like being held by the holy spirit itself.

Inside the cave the peace of its sacredness transcended over me, the visit bought so much more than I ever expected, I said my prayers to Mary Magdalene, feeling her energy and essence there in every section of the cave. Especially in the lower levels where I saw orbs and felt the energy of spirits pass over me. I was lucky enough to video the orbs near the statute of Mary Magdalene and I believe it was there that I received her loving light.

When we came out of the cave it was as if time had stood still, we were alone for several minutes, I just sat outside fully in a trance of bliss and peace until a group of women arrived all dressed in red and I immediately thought a sisterhood of the rose, we were see this group of women later in the evening in Nans le Pins, they too were on their own Divine Feminine Pilgrimage.

After visiting Sainte Baume we went for a meal at Saint Baume Hostelry, Plan-d'Aups and the running waters of nearby. The woodland is full of oak trees and these sacred trees don't often grow in this area of France, they are full of ancient knowledge and wisdom and the oak leaf and acorn are long associated with Magdalene.

We also visited Saint Maximin where the Skull of Mary Magdalene is within a crypt, all set in gold, you go down a few stairs into a crypt room to see the skull and festivals it is bought out and set up as this photo. It felt very sacred, holy and the Basilica is very old and well worth visiting. We lit candles there to our mothers' in heaven and felt the peace of this holy place.

We also went to Sainte Maries de la Mer and stayed there for a few days, visiting the church and flamingo wild park. We swam in the sea and dreamt of what it would have been like to arrived there in over 2000 years ago when it was a small fishing port.

Mary Magdalene along with her family, friends and followers landed in the South of France sometime after the crucifixion, she was among two other Marys, Lazarus and Martha and others. They landed a small fishing village near Marseilles in the Camargue area of France, this village was called Oppidum- Ra or Ra after the Roman occupation and later its name changed to Notre Dame of Ratis and then to Sainte Maries De La Mer.

They landed in a rudderless boat on the shores, or their boat had lost its way over the Mediterranean seas. They landed and began their new life in France. With her companions she became the first preachers of the Gospel in Provence, they travelled around the area and preached at Marseilles, Carcassonne and other areas and lived for several years in the cave or grotto at Sainte Baume.

It is said that she was expelled from Palestine with her disciples in the persecutions against the Christians after Jesus's ascension. They left in a boat and lost their way and landed in Provence. Mary travelled with Mary Salome and Mary of Clopas and these three women were with

Jesus after his crucifixion and when he ascended, Mary Magdalene is mentioned in the New Testament as being the first person to see him when the tomb was empty. The three Maries set sail from Alexandria, Egypt with Joseph of Arimathea there were others in their party who came and settled in France.

Mary Salome was the daughter of Saint Anne, the half sister of the Virgin Mary and she was the wife of Zebedee. Zebedee and Mary had at least two sons who were disciples. Mary Salome is mentioned in Matthew 27:56 Zebedee was a fisherman and is mentioned a few times in the New Testament in Matthew and Mark and he lived near Bethsaida.

Mary of Clopas was also at the crucifixion and was known as one of the three Marys at the tomb of Jesus and who landed in France. Mary of Clopas is mentioned in John 19:25 as being with the women present at the crucifixion.

Now there stood by the cross of Jesus His mother, and His mother's sister, Mary of Clopas, and Mary Magdalene. Also, in the Gospels of Mark and Matthew

Among which was Mary Magdalene, and Mary the mother of James and Joseph, and the mother of Zebedee's children. (Matthew 27:56)

There were also women looking on afar off: among whom was Mary Magdalene, and Mary the mother of James the less and of Joses, and Salome. (Mark 15:40)

(I am not sure if Joses and Joseph are the same person as this would sit better with my understanding of the two Gospels)

So, these three Marys were part of Jesus's following, they

are mentioned several times in the Gospels there is some consistency in the Gospels and it seems strange that there are three Marys so this does add to some confusion. Yet it is clear these women Jesus's Mother, Mary Magdalene his companion, Mary Salome, his Aunt and Mother's sister and Mary Clopas or Cleophas.

It is not clear if Mary was the wife of Clopas or daughter of Clopas, but there are some indications that she might have been related to Mary (Mother of Jesus) another Aunt, but from my research, it's not fully clear. (I shall have to channel with Jesus and Mary to find out some more about this)

It is believed that Mary Magdalene had a daughter called Sarah and she is Saint Sarah, she is celebrated by the gipsies on her Feast Day 24th May at Saint Maries de la Mer. She is also called Sara-la-Kali and she is a black saint; she was either one of Magdalene's servants or followers or her daughter. Her statue is in the church at Saint Maries de la Mer. Her name Sara la Kali means Sarah the Black.

I have had visions of being there with the Marys, part of the following, on the boat and landing and living in France, my memories included being around Jesus before and after the crucifixion as a young girl. These visions came to me whilst I was studying for my High Priestess Course and included later visions of being in the hills probably the Pyrenees and drowning in a deep pool. It is a sad past life because I believe I was out collecting things or part of a group travelling and I had let my mistress Mary Magdalene down by losing my life in this way.

The Camargue Cross

We visited the Camargue area and stayed near the sea for a few nights on how Magdalene Holiday (Pilgrimage) we swam in the sea and visited the Notre- Dame de la Mer Church was built in the 12th Century it looks a bit like a fortress. The Camargue area is so different from Provence, it is full of lagoons, home to horses, farms and flamingos.

It has fields upon fields of sunflowers in the summer months and its symbol is the Camargue Cross, this is a symbol of the Latin cross with upper ends that represent the three-pronged fork and a lower end to represent the sea anchor with a heart to represent the Maries.

The cross for faith,
The anchor for hope,
The heart for love.

The Camargue cross was created by the painter and sculptor Hermann Paul in 1924 at Marquis of Baroncelli's request. The first one, forged in 1930 and was put in Saintes-Maries-de-la-Mer, near the Maure bridge not far from the Simbeu farmhouse where the Marquis of Baroncelli used to live. Today, it is still there.

Every May 25th, the Feast of the Three Marys, Les Gardians carry the relics of Saint Mary Jacobe and Saint Mary Salome on horseback to the sea along with their Camargue Cross.

You will often see this cross either in gold or black on logos etc for Mary Magdalene, her other symbols are red, a skull, an alabaster jar for anointing and she is often shown with an Egyptian Ankh.

Timeline of Sainte Baume

47 AD the arrival of Mary Magdalene and her followers, family and friends

415 AD Saint Jean Cassien created his first priory after returning from Egypt

1279 Charles II of Anjoy, conducts excavations which lead to the discovery in Saint- Maximin of the Mary Magdalene Relics

1295 Charles II invites the Dominicans in Saint Maximin and La Sainte Baume

1695 Pope Urban VIII creates the fraternity Mary Magdalene

22 Days Guidance

Each day you will connect with your beliefs of self, of ego stories, experiences, that separate you from the whole from your Joy and Abundance.

If you don't feel Joyful and Abundant all the time, over this course you being a new journey into dissolving all aspects of lack, resistance to feeling fully Joyful and Abundant to change your patterns, behaviours and beliefs.

Desire
You need to desire to change your thoughts your beliefs to step into the new perception of health, wealth, love, joy, happiness etc.

Commitment
Make a commitment to yourself to listen to the daily meditations and spend some time focusing on your blockages to living a full joyful abundant life.

Get Ready it Begins with You

Say I am ready

Consistency

I know you all have busy lives, you just need 20 mins to listen to the Meditations and a few minutes to connect to the Starchild card and read the Step Intentions.

Try to connect everyday this makes the dissolving work better, but it not listen to what you can. The meditations are recorded so you can listen watch them on replay.

Detachment

You must detach from desired outcomes of how you would like your happiness to be, how you want your abundance to be, just allow the natural flow of Joyful Abundance to come to you and be part of the new you in your new life.

Follow the Program

Follow each step of the program you can see the plan on page ..... you can listen to the First Meditation on Day one and at any other time you feel guided to. Each day there will be a different chakra to connect to for 7 days then you repeat for the whole 22 days.

Alternative Program

You can is you wish do this course over 8 weeks instead of 22 days, by following one chakra rose after another for a week at a time, eg week one Pink Bliss, week two Ruby Red Rose. This format would take longer but would fit into a busy lifestyle and you would have seven days on each meditation instead of the three following the course.

Remember the MP3s are available free from www.orarosetemple.com

Daily Plan 22 Days

Day One

Mary Magdalene Pink Bliss
Introduction - Pink Rose

One of the limitless possibilities for your own personal growth. It is a number that pushes you to look at your current circumstances and see that you have the power to turn your life into anything you wish, today embrace all things new.

Thank you for accepting my invitation to take this Journey with me, you will have many guides and helpers that will support you on this Journey. Mary Magdalene, Anandamayi Ma, Kwan Yin and Mother Mary. Each month this year we have been in so much deep reflection and push pull energies with our ascension into 5 Dimension and beyond, our lives have changed so much during this year.

You may have felt the energies of the higher realms of 5 Dimension as it is pulsating towards us each day and the extremes of clinging to 3 Dimension paradigms and you will have tested. I have so no doubt this would have happened to you.

If you felt like your life has been a rollercoaster. These daily meditations will help you to centre each day, anchor your light and dissolve your resistances to change.

There has been this intensity of letting go of the old stories, the old experiences and stepping into the new. Self care is one of the things that you may have heard day after day, look after yourself, and love yourself. You may receive lots of new creative ideas during this time, you might not do them all but your creativity will be unlocked and with that energy will bring the Abundance and Joy we seek.

You are becoming
You are Self Love
Look at all you are
Have done
Look at yourself

Kim Ora Rose

Energy is the one of most important commodities in your life, not electric or gas, I mean your core energy of life that you use every day. The energy you have as human being living an experience on earth. It is the vibration that radiates from you. You may have read or heard about 3rd Dimension and 5th Dimension vibrations and know that we are shifting from a 3D perspective to a 5D reality, the earth is changing its vibrations and we are too. This can be challenging but its happening and we are having the ride of our lives. You may have felt the deepest reflection of yourself recently and the deepest love of all creation. These are both aspects of the moving forward. Many of our thoughts are from our childhood and family conditioning, and those are filtered through into our own beliefs. One analogy I've been using is that we see the world and our experiences through different lens, sometimes we may have a filter on that lens too. Everything is about perception of what we feel in our lives.

It is these very beliefs that hold us back from experiencing pure Joy and the fullness of Abundance. Positive thoughts can fill our consciousness, raise our vibrations and help us to expand our core energy outwards. Negative thoughts or judgements or feelings of lacking something hold a denser energy they contract us inwards energetically leaving us with a small sphere of influence. They make us tired, irritable, and lost.

This course will help you unlock the negative thoughts and patterns and create new behaviours for your mind, body and soul. Other people in your life be it friends, family, colleagues are affected by our vibrations and you may find they react to us in strange ways. When we raise our vibrations we bring in more Joy, abundance and happiness into our lives. We touch the true essence of being a human being having a human experience on earth. Everything we could ever imagine could be accessible to you.

This might sound too easy and it is, during these 22 days you will begin to unlock joy and abundance in your life.

During this first meditation you will connect with Mary Magdalene's Pink Bliss Ray with the soft pink rose. I received this energy when I visited Sainte Baume Cave in Provence, France on the Summer Solstice in 2019. It is the most peaceful, blissful energy I have ever felt and this is within the first meditation for Day one and you can listen to anytime you wish to be in this loving peaceful energy, it brings you to zero point of purest love. Pink

Bliss Ray of Light channelled by Kim Ora Rose 2019.

You might like to buy the 22 Days Journal to accompany this course it is designed with pages for each day for you to record your experiences. It is available on www.orarosetemple.com or Amazon

Paperback Internationally

https://www.amazon.co.uk/dp/B0BCRXJN2F

Dance in the water
of life
Connect to all that is
Beautiful
Be within the joy
of everything

Kim Ora Rose

Meditation with Pink Bliss & Mary Magdalene

Go into yourself, breathe, go within, step beneath the veil inside

Surround yourself with Pink Mist Light
Allow it to flow around your feet,
Your ankles, knees, your thighs
Your body, root chakra, up to your sacral chakra
Up to your Solar Plexus and on to your heart
Pause there and see a pink rose forming
Step into your Pink Rose
Be at one with your Pink Rose
Feel the petals
The softness of the Petals
You are the beautiful Pink Rose
Feel all the peace and bliss from the pink rose within you
Spend some time in this beautiful soothing, supporting energy of Self Love

Feel the presences of Mary Magdalene join you
First you sense her heavenly perfume coming towards you
Then you see her with your spiritual eyes
Then you feel the touch of her gentle hands
Holding yours for sometime

Blessings flow from her to you
She gives you a Key a Golden Ankh
This is the Key to unlock your endless Joy and Abundant Heart

Breathe deeply and deeply going into the Pink Bliss energy
Going deeper and deeper into the Pink Mist
See yourself surrounded by the Pink Bliss

Feel it melt away all your fears, worries, anxiety
Feel the pink bliss loving energy surround you
Fully be the Bliss energy
You are the Bliss energy it is you

Spend some time in this energy

Come back when you feel ready
You are ready to begin this journey into your heart

Day One Rose Journey Pink Bliss Rose

Describe what did you experience today from the teachings, meditation etc?

Day Two

Root Chakra Meditation with Mary Magdalene & Ruby Ray Rose

In this chapter we explore your thoughts about money and abundance and how they frame your life experiences.

Read these two statements and do any of them ring true to you? If the first statement relates to you, this the mind programming from the old paradigm from our parents and grandparents when they lived through difficult times, if you relate to the second statement of limitless, full of love and life is abundant you are looking at the world and your experience in the new ways. This approach is much healthier and you experience more happiness and contentment in your life.

"Life isn't easy
You have to work hard for money
If only I had more money
Money is the root of all evil"
(Old Paradigm)

Life is abundant
Limitless
Full of Love
Be that Love

Be full of limitless abundance
(New Earth)

There are three aspects attitudes for this root chakra healing the first is Money, second is Fear and third is Safety/Security. When I first wrote this course last year fear and safety were not two aspects I was particularly worried about but during this pandemic they are deep emotions that have arisen in myself worrying about myself and others and these are daily in the news in our country. So we will explore these aspects to release our resistance to feel fully safe and let fears go during these three days in the program.

Where does Fear sit with you?
How does is come in?

I believe we should all allow ourselves to feel each of our emotions and know them, so that as they arise we recognise them and can bring ourselves back to zero point, to be centred, to be neutral and it all takes practice. So as we recognise how each emotion makes us feel, where it sits in us eg in our root, in our hearts in our minds and then we can feel it acknowledge it and breath into each emotion letting them go.

Where does the emotion of safety and basic needs sit with you? For many of us it sits in our Root Chakra and this emotion has been very important in 2020. In the lockdown we were mainly looking after our essentials, our basic needs and for many of us these have been challenging times, people have lost their jobs, incomes, so will have lost their homes and basic necessities of life have been challenged to say the least.

So on our pursuit of ascension we are being pushed and pulled between the 3D reality of living and the 5 D reality of the new world, the new earth, we feel it in our essence, our souls remind us constantly that we are pure love and therefore it is time to explore our resistances and blockages that may have arisen over the last few months to fully awaken to more abundance in our lives.

In your lives there can be the constant struggle about money, fears and safety subconsciously you may feel you have to work hard for money, it is hard to receive money, you struggle to earn enough or you spend too much. You may feel your whole life as been challenged, turned around and uprooted. This conditioning is passed down to through your family and ancestors and embedded by experiences of life and people in your life.

You may find it hard to discuss money, fears and safety with others and this is normal for many of you. Many people feel that others don't want to listen to these fears and worries as when we tell others how we feel they feel that they have to help us and don't know how. So they react to what we are saying.

Many of you will have heard your Grandparents voices to you about money and your parents/guardians. Our grandparents lived through times of war and they would have experienced times of deep worry too. These are words of the 3D paradigm we are moving away from this way of thinking, believing, living, knowing etc. There is a huge shift happening right now on the planet and it begins with you, us. We are all in this together. In this year we have been challenged more so than since the second world war, depending on where you live in the world you have had experienced suffering too. Have you ever felt guilty for having a good job, a good wage, having money given to you, having a nice car, or house?

Perceptions about money can affect your life. The ego has a big role in your experiences, your happiness, the joy you feel each day and the role of money in your life. Each of you will have a different perception about money different values, belief systems, behaviours and patterns. Even if you a steady flow of money coming into your life, as a salary or commission, you still get the feelings of what ifs, what if it stops, what if I lost this flow of money? I have to save for a rainy day? Etc You can get into the fear based thinking about never having enough money or energy, resources, love, health these are all the same when you fear what you might lose you feel that you have something missing this can be part of a mind set.

The simplest way of dissolving not having enough, Fear Worry is through connecting with your wishes and Gratitude. Gratitude is the Key to fulfilment and a massive sign to the universe that you are open to receive, this and feeling the loving rays of the love through the roses and intentions of the Way of Love you will open the doors of lack and fear to change your perceptions and move into full joyful abundance. All abundance and joy issues are particularly connected to your blockages in your root chakra at our base, this is a symbol of red, this is your energy centre where spirit and matter are linked.

The root chakra deals with physical manifestations, located in your lower end of your spines. It is here we connect to aspects of universal energy throughout root to your earth star chakra beneath the ground. If your root chakra is blocked you are cutting off some of your connection to Mother Earth Gaia. The Sanskrit word muladhara for this energy suggests that this is the base of everything. So we begin at the base of everything with this course to Joyful abundance. If your root chakra is blocked you can malfunction, as abundance cannot unfold without support. Feel the loving arms of support around of Mary Magdalene. By feeling your desires and what is missing or lacking in your life you really feel, sense these emotions within you. You can drop the feelings of lacking things that you do not have and fully feel what it is like to have these things.

The ruby ray of love fills you completes and unlocks your blockages, the gratitude tells the universe I am ready to receive more. You are opening yourself up to receive all the blessings of the universe and more, if you are a healer, do some self healing with each of the meditations. Enjoy your day, if anything comes up journal.

Root Chakra Meditation with Mary Magdalene & Ruby Ray Rose

Experience the thoughts and resulting emotions within you that block your abundance in your first root chakra.

See this as a red rose bud. Sit or lay in a comfortable position, your spine straight, erect if sitting, aligned if lying, be relaxed,

Hold the image of a Red Rose Bud in your mind, feel all your resistance to abundance in your life - hold those thoughts that stop you from being fully present eg Life is difficult.

You have to work hard for your money, or Money is the root of all evil. Pause. Hold those thoughts in your mind, feel these fully, they are the blockages within to receiving full abundance. Now open up the Red Rose, image that it holds all you desire, all the things you would like in your life, health, love, happiness, joy, abundance, wealth etc.

See each thought opening up like one of the petals in your hands. Experience them fully with your complete enthusiasm. Recall all your dreams, desires, wishes and all your goals for the future.
Feel this beautiful energy pulsating through your body, aura and being. Now see the Red Rose transform into a soft pink Rose.
Fill your heart, your mind, your aura, your Root Chakra with this gentle loving energy it may come as a mist to you or within the rose form.
Feel all your gratitude in your heart, mind, soul for all you have in your life, everything you own, personal experiences,

friends, loved ones, pets, your home and all you have.
Feel this deeply within and say a few words in your mind
of Gratitude for all you have. Feel it with all your complete
enthusiasm.

Feel the limitless gratitude with you for everything in your
life, your health, your home, your life, love in your life
everything
Come back when you are ready
Enjoy your day - beautiful soul

You may wish to keep a journal of what comes up for you
on this Blessed Day

Mary Magdalene walks
with you each
and
every day

Rose Journey - Ruby Ray Rose

Describe what did you experience today from the teachings, meditation etc?

Day Three

Step Two Sacral Chakra– Orange Rose Ray

When you explore the issues relating to your relationships with family, friends, colleagues and strangers and your expressions of feelings and emotions you are affected by your Sacral Chakra this energy centre activates when you are a child and can be blocked or partially blocked preventing full flow. This area also relates to feelings of sexuality and how you feel about intimate relationship.

The womb or hara space sits here in this energy centre, the giver of creativity and endless possibilities. You can hold deep beliefs, values, behaviours and emotions within this space.

As you connect with your womb space you can connect deeply to Divine Feminime aspects of Mary Magdalene and Kwan Yin as they hold space for you too. Honour your family, friends and guides, ancestors that walk each day with you.

Life begins with water, we are 80% water so they say, so when your waters within your life are not in balance and harmonious you can feel threatened and struggle to express yourself fully. You may hold pains and hurts in your Sacral chakra relating to your childhood, mother/

fatherhood and to your personal intimacy.

The water element also symbolises purification, unconditional love, thoughts and feelings can have a purifying effect when you cleanse and clear your sacral chakra. Joy creativity and happiness can fully flow when you are connected to your sacral chakra and it is fully open.

An authentic expression of true flowing energy can be purified and washed away to dissolve the feelings, emotions of lack, fears and concerns that you face. For true feelings to be expressed in your life you need to learn to be still and listen to distinguish between what is a true feeling of love and what is not.

Which emotions hold true essence of love, joy and which are the demanding wants of the ego always looking for something more?

When you truly feel love with your honesty and true feelings then all of creativity can flow to you. You will see a change in your relationships with other people and dissolving of unnecessary blockages will melt. Experience all resistance, desires and gratitude for all you have.

Listen to the meditation once or twice if you can and remember to journal your experiences with your emotions, feelings, the energy of the colours and anything to see in the meditation. You can spend longer in the meditation to fully go deeper into the energy.

Sacral Chakra Orange Rose Ray with Mother Mary Meditation

Go gently inside,

Let all the thoughts of the day slip away

Breathe and go deeply into a gentle slumber

See yourself in a beautiful flower garden and see all the flowers around you they are all orange in colour, so many different flowers but all shades of orange.

You see a water fountain in the garden and by it stands a figure, walk to wards the fountain an you will see it is Mother Mary standing there in blue.

She holds her hands out to greet you and you feel all her love flow towards you.

Stay there holding hands with Mother Mary whilst to revisit in your mind all your thoughts about feeling your true emotions, your true thoughts, times when you felt you couldn't express them, behaviours and values, some may be family values or cultural/religious values allow those thoughts to form into symbolic tears and give them to Mother Mary, she collects them up and puts them into the fountain where they are cleansed and cleared.

Let go of any thoughts of not being enough, any pain or memories from your childhood with your Mother or Father or your own motherhood/fatherhood and any thoughts about your personal intimacy. Let them flow, give them to Mother Mary and she cleanses them in the fountain.

When you have let everything go, she takes a golden cup and collects some of the water and give you to drink, drink deeply from the cup.

Fully feel all your desires for joy and happiness to be within you, feel all your desires of how you wish your life to be, how you wish your emotions to be

Fully feel everything within you right now,

Mother Mary now gives you an Orange/Coral Rose this means I love you and feel all it energy blend with you, feel it in every cell of your body, every thought is full of love, of joy and feel your true feelings budding within you.

Fully being in this energy of the orange rose as it unfolds within you

Feel gratitude for all the limitless joy and creativity, ways to express yourself unfolding, self confidence to say what you feel

Fully feel all of this with gratitude and happiness

Stay within this energy for as long as you wish

Journal any feelings or visions that come up for you

Rose Journey - Orange Rose Ray with Mother Mary

Describe what did you experience today from the teachings, meditation etc?

Day Four

Step Three Solar Plexus Chakra with Mary Magdalene and Yellow Rose

For abundance to naturally flow to you need to hold the masculine energies of determination to enjoy the fullness and completion in your lives you need to feel the feminine quality of being satisfied with deep heartfelt desires of acceptance. Mary Magdalene come in with her gentle way and the Divine Masculine of balance is needed for full flow of abundance and joy to flow within you. Together with this balance of the DF and DM within you they can bring transformation that can be felt as you channel their energies.

The more energy that flows naturally through the solar plexus the more you will be able to actively engage with life with the power and wisdom that is yours. It is already there within you and you go deeper and deeper into this solar plexus you will see it emerge within your life.

To break out of old patterns, belief systems the meditation will help dissolve your resistance to all that needs to be released for the new 5D energy to fully flow in you. Just be willing to allow this to be released, dissolved, melted away naturally. As you express your desires of self confidence, aligning and igniting your inner power and wisdom, balancing your DF and DM aspects these will flow naturally to you. The gratitude for all you have gives the signal to the cosmos, the universe that you are ready to receive more and the Yellow Rose Ray brings more of Christ's energy to blend with your energy to unlock the riches in your wisdom and power.

Mary Magdalene with Yellow Rose Meditation

Sit in a comfortable position or lie down, keeping your spine straight, relax, your whole body and go within, taking some deep breaths, allowing your shoulders to relax and let go of any tension in your body.

Feel the energy of Mary Magdalene draw close, she brings a Yellow colour of energies for you to feel all the healing from this colour.

Call in your guides or helpers too.

Sense yourself within a beautiful garden full of the most amazing flowers you have very seen they are in different colours go and look some of the flowers that are past their blooming phase and take one in your hands.

As you connect to this flower really experience all your thoughts and emotions that block your flow of abundance and feel them flowing into the flower.

Experience the thoughts and resulting emotions that block the flow of abundance in your sacral chakra, all the ways you feel you are powerless or lack the wisdom you need.

Recall in your mind times when you felt fear and any difficulties about expressing your feelings

Feel all your desires in your life with complete enthusiasm fully feeling all your desires to connect with your inner power, your own wisdom, remember times when you were unsure about your abilities your own power and feel each of these emotions.

Play these out in your mind, express how you feel when you cant express yourself fully and how your body feels if you have to bottle up your emotions.

Now Mary Magdalene comes transforms your flower into a beautiful yellow rose and places it next to your heart, feel all the abundance flowing to you, limitless freedom of flowing abundance being poured into you, in the yello rose ray.

Feel it, feel it all, as it blends with you and you can feel where this energy is flowing throughout your body, aura etc.

Now fully feel all the abundance in your life all your wonderful range of emotions that guide you each day, feel the abundance of your own wisdom, your own inner guidance and the ways you express yourself. Feel all your gratitude for everything in your life. Fully feel each petal of the yellow rose and all it brings to you.

Come back when you feel ready

Enjoy your day and write in your journal all you have received.

If anything comes up during the day remember to write about it your journal.

Rose Journey with Mary Magdalene and Yellow Rose

Describe what did you experience today from the teachings, meditation etc?

Day Five

Step 4 Heart Chakra Ruby Rose Ray

At this time we are experiencing a desire to heal from our past hurts and pains, as we grow into the ascension of leaving 3D thinking and moving into a 5D reality we are experiencing more and more love in our lives and this love energy brings us closer to Unity. You need an open heart to receive more unity and love and any blockages of pain, suffering, trauma, hurts etc need to be released and healed to move forward with more love.

If you have a closed heart to love you find it hard to express yourself on many levels and the surplus of love that is flowing all around you struggles to penetrate you, it bounces all around you, you will feel it but cant take it into your heart. By clearing your pains, releasing old wounds and hurts, you will open your heart wider to feel the love of creation, love of the cosmos that flows around us all. A closed heart will create inner turmoil, illness, conflict and separation from the whole. If your immune system is weak it can be a sign of a closed heart and if you have a healing crisis it is your body's way of trying to clear out the old pains and hurts. All these show your resistance to love, to feel love, to show love, to accept love from others and the simplest way to dissolve such resistance is by acknowledging it. Abundance does not exist without love, abundance is love, your heart chakra is at the centre of your love in your life. Love is the central energy of the universe. If you wish to experience more love in your life you must be willing to feel all your resistance against love. Really go deep into all of your feelings of unworthiness, your deepest fears of not finding love, of being unworthy of true love, your deepest feelings about betrayal, abandonment, deepest feelings of needing another's' approval and any ideas you may have that negate love.

Examine your fear of vulnerability of how you could be hurt if you opened your heart.

Go into your deepest fears about being embarrassed and confused when confronted with true love. Feel those feelings of unfamiliarity of hindrance of some sort of imminent danger. Feel how you reject love and how you are absolutely starved of love, because you daren't open up to love in your life. If you are open enough to feel your resistance and desire for love, this true and unconditionally love will reveal itself to you. This is the Bliss energy of Pure Love I talk about in the mediations and in Day One of this journey, it will show its self to you, if may come in white or pink or another colour but it is waiting for you to experience it.

Love doesn't happen to you.
You don't need to depend on outside sources
of others to feel this Love.
Feeling Love is within you
At your core you are Love
Creation is Love
Limitless Love is within you

All issues of true love, of empathy within living things

are closely related to the opening of this energy centre because it is here where the more physical and emotional forces of the lower energy centres meet the higher energy centres. That is why we have the two colours of Green and Pink for the heart chakra. Take the white from the upper chakras and the red from the root and together here at the heart you have pink of True Love. Self Love.

All that is Love

Whenever there is a marriage of higher and lower chakras true unconditional love unfolds, like the rose bud, it unfolds petal by petal as it blooms, like all flowers, trees, plants they unfold, embracing and penetrating true unconditional love into all aspects of being, transforming the worldly into the Divine. You are the Divine, you are the I AM Divine aspect of all that is. Where there used to be judgements and separation there is acceptance with this heightened perception and discrimination. Negative emotions cannot prevail over love. Whenever you attend lovingly to your anger or despair, sadness, feeling them fully they will quickly dissolve as if vanished into thin air. Loving your illness also promotes healing. When you love your illness for the message it is sending you or the lesson it wants show you a healing takes place.

This love I felt after leaving Saint Baume in Provence the Mary Magdalene Grotto, I've felt it before but this was so profound, I've felt in my husbands' heart, in the eyes of my children. I've felt it whisper to me in Repton's Church Crypt in Derbyshire, from Andressey Island near the River Trent, with ancient words from the early Christians and in the waters at the Chalice Well.

Mary Magdalene has guided me to write and and share this course with you and if you are reading this right now, know that you have been guided to fully connect with Mary Magdalene's loving essence. This is the energy of True Love, Bliss and it will awaken within you as you connect with its energy. Unconditional love is the highest form of abundance there is and very healing too.

You will be joined by Mother Mary in this meditation she brings her love too.

Heart Chakra Ruby Rose Ray Meditation

Sit in a comfortable position, or lie with your spine straight, relax
Breathe into each breath fully, feeling the air flow into you body into your lungs and feel it as you exhale

Fully feeling each breath, breath by breath relax

Notice anywhere that is in discomfort, direct your breath to that area and relax

Fully relax

See yourself on a golden beach with the warm sun, soft sand beneath your feet and the sea waves gently lapping the shore line.

A beautiful sea gull lands by your side and invites you to explore your feelings about unconditional love

As you connect to the sea gull, notice is feathers, its features and see the beauty within the bird

Now notice yourself, your body, your heart, where are you holding on to not allowing love to flow, where do you have resistance to love in your life, what does love feel like, feel it now and see where you have been blocking it out in your life.

Experience fully with your completeness how you do not fully open up to unconditional love, when someone pays you a compliment how do you react, do you thing no that's not true, do you accept the compliment?

Fully feel how you are holding back feel this in each breath

Fully own it that you are not fully open to receive love

Now see a figure walking towards you it is Mother Mary she is dressed in blue and white, she brings a small bouncing puppy and it is so alive with desire and love.

As she approaches you feel your heart open wider and wider and when she arrives she holds your hand and guides you to feel all the love of the universe, flowing freely to you, feel this love, follow it , where does it go, where does it end, feel your aura expanding with love wider and wider and wider, where their is only love.

This is your true self a being of love, fulfilled with love

Explore where you let down your control to be loved in a way your thought you should be loved

Play out in your mind incidents when you have compromised yourself to gain approval from another. Feel these emotions rising and let them flow from you.

Mother Mary offers you the loving puppy with all its joy and bountiful energy and you feel its love flow to you, she invites you to let go of all resistance to love and asks you to place all your resistance into a red shell, the moment your old patterns are released to the shell they are transformed into ruby ray roses which Mother Mary gives back to you.

You place these red roses in a hair garland or around your neck, or in what ever way feels right for you.

Now feel all the gratitude for all the loving experiences in your life with your family, friends, pets, loved ones.

Fully feel this love flowing fully thought-out yourself, in each breath there is only love and you fully feel it.

Let your feelings of love and gratitude fully touch everything and everyone you meet today.

Mother Mary holds your hands and your heart cleansing is complete today, she places her hand on your heart with a seal of love.

Spend more time in this blissful place if you wish and visit often.

Journal Everything that comes up for you

Rose Journey Ruby Rose Ray with Mother Mary

Describe what did you experience today from the teachings, meditation etc?

Day Six

Step Five Express Yourself - Throat Chakra, Blue Rose Ray

Mary Magdalene often comes with the Pink Rose and the Blue Rose you may read different things about what these two roses mean and for me the Blue Rose is about truth and speaking from your truth. Mary Magdalene spoke out about her truth and her ways of healing and of love and you will find these messages at the core of all her teachings, her wisdom, love, healing and truth. All communication issues are connected to the throat chakra to blockages in this chakra and this is wear sounds originate.

The throat chakra acts as a bridge from the heart to the 3rd eye and crown chakras and its is one that is often blocked or cracked too wide open. Sometimes we can not say enough and sometimes too much. In order for complete abundance to flow we need to be fully open and aware of how we reach in each situation and on these days we will really be looking at how you express yourself in different situations.

Try to recall times when you felt you couldn't say anything and times when you said too much. Times when you have guarded your words, times when you wished you had said more, or less. Observe what and who you are protecting and what are you hiding from others. What are you trying to hide from yourself.

As your live experiences grow you will see things from different points of view and this is one of life's great teachings to see from different perspectives and see the truth in many things for what is truth for one person might not be for another. In seeing these many truths we do not limit ourselves from being from only one point of view and can see the many aspects of life, the many facets in the diamond and the two sides or more to every situation. In this we can fully be in unity with our brothers and sisters, with our compassion and unison of love for everyone.

As you connect to Mary Magdalene, Divine Council of Light, Ascended Masters, Angels and other light beings you will learn more about this wisdom, these perspectives of truth and the ways that others view the world in realising that there are many truths and it depends on who's eyes you are seeing from. This becomes part of the link between the throat chakra and the 3rd eye as the two are so linked. True communication comes when you can fully listen, by learning to listen to others, you can fully find the purist of communication.

You can listen to others and understand them more, what they are saying, what they are hiding and what they really mean. When you are in communication with Source you know the truth, you can fully communicate and speak at the right time or walk away.

Communication is an important aspect of abundance when we speak of our intentions from true Self, the

Universe reacts, the Law of Attraction is set in motion, in the material realms of our physical lives abundance is a result of our actions with others. You will notice when you are positive about something then positive things come to you.

Meditation with Blue Rose Ray & Mary Magdalene

Sit in a comfortable position, or lie with your spine straight, relax

Breathe into each breath fully, feeling the air flow into you body into your lungs and feel it as you exhale

Fully feeling each breath, breath by breath relax

Notice anywhere that is in discomfort, direct your breath to that area and relax

And fully relax

See a blue mist around you, feel it flowing all around you,

See the mist starting to disperse and as you do so step out into the new landscape, it is fill with blue light, you are in a garden full of blue trees, blue flowers, blue butterflies and walk around the garden exploring everything that is blue, so many shades, hues of blue. Call in Mary Magdalene to join you in this beautiful place.

Before you there is a blue water fountain, see the water flowing in its blue shades of light - Mary invites you to take a drink from the fountain.

Hold your hands under the flowing water, it feels so inviting,

Take a cup and drink from the fountain

Drinking in the blue light, the blue water

Feel it fully in your throat chakra, opening up with the blue water

Sit for a moment fully feeling your resistance to being fully in your truthful light, now you resist to be fully open with others and how you fear rejection and opinions if you speak your truth.

Fully remember when you have said to much and where that emotion sits within you.

Drink again from the fountain and feel your throat chakra area opening up to more and more blue light.

Now fully embrace everything you desire connected to your communications, to fully hear everything, to understand the truth of a situation, to fully be able to express yourself by word, voice, song, written words etc.

Now Mary steps closers and speaks to your Soul, she whispers in her own language the words of love to you.

If you seek to speak light language feel yourself fully being able to do this
Really desire all you wish to be in full abundance, see yourself writing your course, books, poems, artwork, see yourself as the artist, author, poet, speaker

See yourself as you wish to be seen in full abundance it is yours

See the blue light flowing through you with more and more abundance, freeing you from your doubts, from your fears.

Feel all of creation within your throat chakra when communication is fully opened to you.

Now take another drink from the fountain and really embrace all that you have, give gratitude to your expression, to your confidence, to your vocabulary, to your creativity

Fully be in gratitude in your past, present and future in every communication,

Let the attitude of gratitude touch you when ever you communicate your true feelings during the day

When you feel ready bring yourself back see the blue rose in our hand

Rose Journey Intuition with Blue Rose Ray

Describe what did you experience today from the teachings, meditation etc?

Day Seven

Step Six 3rd Eye Intuition with Indigo Moonlight Rose

Intuition and inner knowing are particularly connected to the 3rd eye, you receive information from all of your chakras and especially when you receive gut instincts from your Solar Plexus and messages from God or Source through your Crown Chakra, but we usually relate to your 3rd Eye for intuition. Through your 3rd eye all five senses combined with the sixth sense of awareness penetrate the outer and inner worlds. This chakra is the wisdom eye, of inner knowing which evolves a more broad and continuous participation in the life's unfolding.

Inner knowing, intuition and conscious awareness are the seeds of manifestation. This energy centre links to the consciousness of the universe it has the power to create new realities to dissolve the structures supporting relating as we know it.

The Sanskrit word for this energy centre is ajna, which means command and control. The ordinary levels of reality symbolised by the root, sacral chakra, solar plexus, heart, throat chakras are controlled by and receive commands from the third eye. Although this can be associated with the pineal gland, this function of command and control is further stressed by the close connection between the 3rd eye and the pituitary gland which also governs the endocrine system.

The capacity of unlocking realms of experience "right here" that are in any ordinary sense "not in this time and space" an abundance of intuition and inner knowing points forward and expresses the inherent unity of all things in true self. Therefore the degree of intuition and inner knowing we enjoy shows how much we are in touch or out of touch with our true nature. The more we are in touch with ourselves the more knowledge can flow through and manifest within us.

One world to the wise, this process of opening up to more and more knowledge flowing through you, cannot be controlled as in the ordinary approach of ego, collecting, hoarding information, instead it happens due to a sudden or gradual surrender to the knowledge which is already there. This surrender proceeds gently enough to naturally protect you against becoming overwhelmed by an overload of "telepathic" information. Intuition will reveal exactly what needs to be known in any given moment. Thus you do not have to do anything or protect yourself.

Since intuition is always available the only thing you need to do in order to unlock its potential is to feel your resistance and desire for it and gratefully accept that which is already there within you. This is your birthright you can enjoy abundance by feeling your limits of what you have been programmed to receive.

Inner knowing comes in different ways, you will have

heard about the different Clairs, the different ways that you receive information, through inner seeing, inner knowing, inner feelings, etc and you will have your main ways of receiving messages from spirit, the different ways your process what you sense. You will find that your favourite ways will change and develop over time. I used to see in my mind and feel alot, then for a time the feeling part left me and I started to receive in new ways, more inner knowing, rather than the feeling. You can think you are losing your abilities, losing your tools but your guides and higher self are showing you more and more ways to sense, feel, know energy and you are growing.

When I started listening and connecting to spirit this was as a child and I saw things, I saw my Grandmother in spirit and saw fairies and secrets. I didn't realise that it was only me that saw these things until I was older. I learnt that I was good with cards at interpreting the patterns I learnt to read the playing cards at around 9 years old, I was good at listening to the sounds in the garden, in the home etc. Also as an empath knowing what others were feeling and sensing emotions. My two dominant ways of receiving information were through clairvoyance inner vision and sensing feeling (clairsentience).

Over time these ways of receiving information more and more ways to receive came to me. We can explore each of the ways to receive information and practise using these different ways. Information is always flowing from spirit, from our guides, higher self etc on different vibrational frequencies of light, they come in like radio waves and you can learn how to change the frequency to hear different beings of light. Some people receive via psychic channels, some via mediumship, channelling and others through different ways.

A bit more about the different Clairs:

Clairvoyance means clear seeing.
This is when visions past, present and future flash through our mind's eye, or third eye, much like a daydream. Many of us are highly visual and able to understand an idea best when we see it written or sketched out as an image on a computer screen or on a canvas. Visual people often choose to be artists, builders, photographers, decorators, designers and so forth. If this sounds familiar, your clairvoyance is most likely a dominant sense.

Clairaudience means clear hearing.
This is when we hear words, sounds or music in our own mind's voice. On rare occasions, spirit may be able to create audible sound, though this takes a tremendous amount of focused energy. Some of us best retain and comprehend information when we hear it spoken aloud. Our natural talents tend to lie in our auditory faculties, often making us gifted musicians, singers, writers and public speakers. If this feels right to you, clairaudience may be a leading sense for you.

Clairsentience means clear feeling.
This entails feeling a person's or spirit's emotions or feeling another's physical pain. Many of us are clairsentient without consciously being aware of it. When we get a strong "gut" feeling, positive or negative, about someone we just met or when we get the "chills" for no apparent reason, we may be tuning into the emotional energy of a person or a spirit around us. When we are

highly sensitive and are in tune with not only our own feelings, but also the feelings of others, this makes us natural healers and caregivers. We often feel inspired to pursue careers as doctors, therapists, counselors, nannies and teachers. If this is you, clairsentience is at the top of your senses list.

Clairalience means clear smelling.
This is being able to smell odours that don't have any kind of physical source. Instances of this could include smelling the perfume or the cigarette smoke of a deceased relative, used as a sign of their presence around us. When our sense of smell is strong and distinct, we may find that certain smells connect us to past memories or we may be drawn to working as a florist, a wine taster or a perfume fragrance creator.

Clairgustance means clear tasting.
This is the ability to taste something that isn't actually there. This experience oftentimes comes from out of the blue when a deceased loved one is attempting to communicate a memory or association we have with a particular food or beverage that reminds us of them. If we have a heightened sense of taste, this would make us natural chefs, bakers or food critics.

Claircognizance means clear knowing.
This is when we have knowledge of people or events that we would not normally have knowledge about. Spirit impresses us with truths that simply pop into our minds from out of nowhere. An example of this would be a premonition: a forewarning of something that will happen in the future. Claircognizance requires tremendous faith because there's often no practical explanation for why we suddenly "know" something.

Many philosophers, professors, doctors, scientists, religious and spiritual leaders and powerful sales and business leaders tend to be highly intuitive and seem to just know the facts with a sense of certainty. If this is you, consider claircognizance as one of your dominant senses.

I found that when I hear or sense now it is so light and I have to trust that is what I need to hear, give etc. Trust is a huge part of this spiritual journey and as you trust and go with the flow of what is coming to you, more and more will come to you.

For this meditation we are going to connect to the beautiful feminine of the full moon energies to really connect to our intuition, in the moonlight our 3rd eye can fully open and you can really sense so much.

A few weeks ago I was connecting with my Twin Flame or Soul particle and he is called "Artun" he is a like a wizard, resides between the dimensions, between the worlds and comes in purple, he is like a magician, a wizard and I wish to bring him into this meditation for you. He is so much about this time where we are in 2020 preparing for the astrological alignment of the yule time. I am sure he will wish to be part of your 3rd clearing and opening whenever you connect with him as he is here as a guide for our time of now.

When he comes in the meditation he is dressed in purple with golden stars, I see him as Arabic or similar in his appearance you may see him differently. It is all as it should be, he is interested in the stars, astronomy and will bring you messages from the universe.

It will be interesting in your feedback to know how he

comes to you and what messages he brings to you. If you feel like sharing that would be fantastic.

3rd Eye Intuition Indigo Moon Rose Meditation with Artun Mystic Guide

Sit in a comfortable position, or lie with your spine straight, relax
Breathe into each breath fully, feeling the air flow into you body into your lungs and feel it as you exhale

Fully feeling each breath, breath by breath relax

Notice anywhere that is in discomfort, direct your breath to that area and relax

fully relaxing

Allow yourself to be surrounded by a deep indigo mist and allow it to flow fully to you, see yourself on a small boat, sailing through the mists and you will arrive at small dock area.

As the mists clears step out onto the shoreline.

You at once see you are on a magical beach, on a tropical shoreline, it is dark, you look up and see the full moon, the moon is so bright,

Walk around the shore, feel the sand, pebbles beneath your feet, hear the sound of the water on the shore, hear the sound of fish in the sea,

Fully sense everything - sound, sight, feelings, emotions, hearing everything

What can you hear?
What can you see?
What do you feel?

What emotions do you have?
What do you sense?

This is a place of wonder, a safe beach lit by moon light

You see the outline of a castle on the horizon with interesting turrets and walls, make your way to the castle, you see a figure on the top of the walls, a man dressed in deepest purple you see the colours first in your mind and then in your inner eyes, you know this colour, you see it when the moonlight shines on his robe.

He sends a direct message to you via his telepathy and you sense it straight away, it is a message of hope, of inner knowing and brings you so much joy.

Sense this now.....

You are still making your way to the castle, walking or flying or whatever mode of transport you would like until you reach the castle.

Artun is now before the great castle doors he is waiting for you, he gives you an indigo rose.

When you reach the doors he greets you and invites you to go inside the castle, you are guided through the great hall, chambers and up to the top of the castle and invited to look out at the full moon, to the stars,

Artun shows you the stars in the sky, he points out different constellations to you,

He shows how they line up ready for changes in our earthly world

He asks you to let go of all your resistance to fully believing in

the intuition that comes to you, to let go of all your fears that hold you back from being fully open in your intuition.

He gives you time to fully remember when you wished you had used your intuition in the past and any emotions that are attached to this.

He says pour all these thoughts, memories, fears into a cup that he holds out for you, and you see each be received in the form of small daisies, each memory is a daisy, each fear a daisy and you fill up the cup with your daisies.

When you have fully released all your fears and thoughts into many daisies, Artun throws them up into the sky and they are transformed into star dust and he give you a cup of star dust, These are so full of potential.

Now think about every desire you have to be fully abundant, how much you want your inner knowing to expand, how you would like your intuition to grow and for you to fully trust all your receive.

Consider the ways you might like your inner wisdom to come to you, do you wish to hear more, feel more, know more.

Feel an abundance of inner knowing within you, for it is fully within you

If you wish to receive more messages from light beings, feel that now, if you wish to receive a stronger connection to Mary Magdalene to Jesus, to God, to the Angels or Divine Councils feel that now as if you have a hot line to them. Feel their love and messages flow directly to you now.

If you wish to speak with light language or connect more to the Lemurians, Arcturians, Sirians, Pleidians, Dragons etc Ask for this now and fully feel the energies of connecting to them.

Spend a few minutes with Artun he can show you how to connect to different dimensions, different vibrations of energies etc.

Ask to be shown how to receive inner knowing and intuition from your higher self, from your Soul and he will show you and deepen that connection.

When you feel ready leave the castle

Thank Artun for his teachings, for his wisdom, knowledge and for sharing his indigo rose and other gifts with you.

Fully feel all your gratitude for everything you have received and for everything you have in your life.

Gratitude for your inner knowing

Feel your gratitude for all your past, present and future experiences

When you feel ready return to the here and now

Enjoy your day

Journal everything for there is meaning in your meditations

Rose Journey Intuition with Indigo Moon with Artun Mystic Guide

Describe what did you experience today from the teachings, meditation etc?

Day Eight

Step 7 Crown Chakra, Divine I AM energy
with Mary Magdalene & Council of Light -
Open up to your True Self - White Rose

Enlightenment and finding it, this chakra is all about opening your crown chakra to receive more enlightenment, to feel the limitless, endless, no form, Divine Being that you are.

You are the Divine I AM energy
You are connected to all things
All things You Are

Nothing much can be said about enlightenment – even Buddha is silent about it, he smiled when asked and showed a flower. I give you a Rose Flower or a Lotus Flower as a symbol of enlightenment, its the pure state where the ego dissolves and you realise you are the All that is, you are the Divine of the Universe, the Universe resides in you. You are stardust. I connect Mary Magdalene, Jesus, Goddess Isis and many others in the Council of Light, a collective consciousness of beings who send us teachings, messages and wisdom as we open up our crown chakras to receive more from the universe, cosmos. One of their clear messages is one of Being, just to be, at peace, calm, with peace of mind within the awaken state of pure being, pure Bliss.

If you have not thoughts or wanting anything you are in this perfect state of just being. At Peace with everything. Anandmayi Ma spoke often about this sense of pure Joy being. Knowing yourself being at peace with yourself being at one with everything and yourself.

Ascension and enlightment are the energies behind us fully being our true selves, after we clear our old patterns, release our old energies. As we fully connect to our crown and higher chakras we connect fully to the limitless energies of Divine Beings. We are each unique divine beings and when you fully connect to your crown chakra you fully feel this. It is hard to explain enlightment it can be like the Buddha says being silent just doing nothing, being no-thing, this is enlightment, when we stop trying to do things, we are just be-ing our divine selves.

We are likened to the lotus flower or the rose, we are beauty itself and we know that this is what we are. When we have dropped the soul searching for finding ourselves, finding our purpose, finding what makes us happy, we find it there in ourselves it was there all along, we dont need the fancy job, the new car, the purpose, at our core, our true self we are enlighted in just being. We feel this in meditation, this sense of joy in being in the now.

Finding this perfect state of being can be by being in the heart, being in our own essence, our zero point, perfect balance and there is one thing that more of us have experience this year is time. We have had more time to be, just be and this helps us on our ascension path, to be at peace. That's when you shut off the fear of a virus, fear of a vaccine, fear of death, illness etc. We each have our own triggers around our fears and you may have found that you have different opinions to others, this is all part of the same truth, the different ways we perceive our lives, our different experiences from different perspectives. Do not get involved with arguments or disagreements about different opinions as the truth can be different through different eyes.

Stepping into no judgements of others is part of the ascension, stepping away from the dramas. The old ways of 3D patterns playing out that divide us as humans. So we are seeking to let go of our resistance to Just BE, letting go of our difficulty in switching the world out, getting off the rollercoaster of making a living and start being in our lives, connecting deeply to ourselves as our true self. We are going to explore releasing all fears of connecting to the Divine Source of all things and fully experience Joy and happiness in all things.

Connecting to balance, calm, peace and the awaken state of pure bliss. We have two ascended masters as guides with this meditation we have Mary Magdalene and Anandmayi Ma with the white rose. You will go on a journey to the Delphi Temple to meet with the Priestesses and Priests of the white rose garden and receive a light transmission.

When you have completed this meditation you start again with the Root Chakra as you continue to follow each meditation for the full 22 days.

Crown Chakra, Divine I AM energy with Mary Magdalene & Anandmayi Ma Meditation - White Rose

This meditation was channelled to be received with the white rose, in a white Rose Garden with you Mary Magdalene and Anandmayi Ma these two pure essences of love and light wish to bring you a light transmission with the energies of the white rose. To open your crown up to unlimited divinity.

Make yourself comfortable and relax, closing your eyes and going within.

Take some deep breaths and relax

Relax now

Feel yourself becoming more and more relaxed

See yourself surrounded by a white mist, it is so bright and you feel the urge to go deeper into your relaxation, do so now

Fee the white surround you and embrace you and count to 5

1, 2 3 4 5 going deeper and deeper into the white

As the mist clears you see yourself before a greek temple with pillars, before the temple is a garden full of roses, you notice that they are all white, different types of roses, all white, small ones, double ones, all pure white.

As you marvel at the roses, you notice priestesses and priests come to join you, they are dressed in white too.

They guide you into the temple and give you a white rose and garland of white roses which you can either have on your head or around your neck.

As you go into the temple you see figures before the altar, you look down, the floor is white marble and it feels so smooth beneath your feet, the altar is made of white marble too. Notice everything on the altar, the candles the white roses adorn it and see everything else that is there.

The two figures step forward you feel Mary Magdalene's essence straight away, she lifts a veil and shows herself in her true beauty, she feels so powerful, more powerful than you may have experienced before - connect with her energy now and fully feel her energy ....

Anandamayi Ma now steps forward and greets you, smiling, you feel waves of excitement meeting her in this sacred temple. Connect deeply to her too.....

They invite you to stand on a circular area within the temple, you look up and see a shaft of light that flows into the temple.

They draw down the white light and direct it to your crown.

Feel it flowing to you, a light beam of white pure light

It comes in waves of light, beaming down on you

This is a direct light beam of light from Source to you.

Stay in the temple as long as you like

You have received Divine Light and you will notice how your crown connection has widen and opened you up more and more to divine light.

Look around you and see beings of light from the Divine Council of Light they are overseeing everything.

Each time you connect with this meditation you will receive more and more divine light.

And so it is

Bring yourself back

Record in your Journal

Blessed Be

Rose Journey Crown Chakra, Divine I AM energy with Mary Magdalene & Anandmayi Ma - White rose

Describe what did you experience today from the teachings, meditation etc?

Day Nine

Mary Magdalene's Pink Bliss & Ruby Red Rose

Now we begin to go deeper with the same meditation I suggest you connect to Mary Magdalene's Pink Bliss on this day and Ruby Red Meditation. As you go deeper with each of the three weeks you really go deeper into releasing old thought patterns, old programming and outdated ways of living to fully delve into the limitless possibilities of life.

You will notice different things coming up for you to release and let go off relating to each of the chakras and their corresponding emotions. By continuing with the course for the full 22 days you will really embody the healing energies of each flower and its colour with the continuing support of Mary Magdalene. During the past week you will have noticed changes within your thinking patterns, shifts of resistance starting to move and new ways of thinking about your life and yourself. When you go through each of the meditations during this week you will notice how the energy feels deeper this time. Remember to journal everything down and look deeper at everything that comes up for you.

If you listen to the Pink Bliss to set intentions for the next stage it will hold you, support you and guide you forward. Allow Mary Magdalene and her pink roses to come to you and feel her energy envelope you with her love.

The Pink Bliss rose and its loving energy of self love links to your higher heart chakra which sits on your Thymus above your heart below your throat area. It is the area that connects you deeply to your higher self and to your divine self. An area of deep self love.

The intentions for this pink rose are:

I love and accept myself just as I am.
I allow myself to unfold like a rose each
and every day, living in love.

We begin again with the Ruby Red Rose on Day Nine too. So on Day Nine you have two meditations to listen to: Pink Bliss and Ruby Red Rose.

You will really feel the shift in your energies between the White Rose of Day Eight and moving back to the Ruby Red Rose of the Root Chakra, it will be like coming home to yourself a comfortable feeling and it will ground you after you have been working with the upper chakras. So we return to your core, to money, to struggles and you will experience them again and release them. Experience your thoughts to do with abundance and lack in your life.

The energy of the root chakra is:

Living in complete Abundance
Living in love, happiness, wealth and health

Diving into all that Abundance
Means to you

Meditation with Pink Bliss & Mary Magdalene

Go into yourself, breathe, go within, step beneath the veil inside

Surround yourself with Pink Mist Light
Allow it to flow around your feet,
Your ankles, knees, your thighs
Your body, root chakra, up to your sacral chakra
Up to your Solar Plexus and on to your heart
Pause there and see a pink rose forming
Step into your Pink Rose
Be at one with your Pink Rose
Feel the petals
The softness of the Petals
You are the beautiful Pink Rose
Feel all the peace and bliss from the pink rose within you
Spend some time in this beautiful soothing, supporting energy of Self Love

Feel the presences of Mary Magdalene join you
First you sense her heavenly perfume coming towards you
Then you see her with your spiritual eyes
Then you feel the touch of her gentle hands
Holding yours for sometime

Blessings flow from her to you
She gives you a Key a Golden Ankh
This is the Key to unlock your endless Joy and Abundant Heart

Breathe deeply and deeply going into the Pink Bliss energy
Going deeper and deeper into the Pink Mist
See yourself surrounded by the Pink Bliss

Feel it melt away all your fears, worries, anxiety
Feel the pink bliss loving energy surround you
Fully be the Bliss energy
You are the Bliss energy it is you

Spend some time in this energy

Come back when you feel ready

You are ready to begin this journey into your heart

When you listen to the audio you can pause the meditation and go deeper if you wish, allowing yourself to spend longer in the sacred space. You might like to create an altar or sacred space in your home whilst you are doing this course with the different colours and symbols to represent each of the daily intentions.

See yourself with a Ruby Red Rose and bring your attention to how you feel about money, feel your blockages within yourself about how money makes you feel and fully feel them.

If you read back on Day Two you can revisit the concept of the old paradigm, old ways of thinking, worrying and fear patterns etc. You will remember that Gratitude is the key to fulfilment and a sign to the universe that you are ready to receive more. As you journey with each of the roses each day you unlock more and more abundance and joy in your life.
Take your awareness to your root chakra and fully tune it to it, ask yourself where are your blockages to abundance?

What words or emotions arise from this question? Now

fully ground your energies again, take your roots down into the earth and fully connect to Mother Earth, feel the flowing energy of the the earth flow to you.

Hold this energy for a few minutes and give thanks for the earth energies. We return to the base of everything to the root, you might like to connect to trees on this day too.

Walk where there are trees, the Yew Tree is particular helpful for getting to the Root of things, it is poisionous but a beautiful tree. Wear red today too, eat some red foods and really embrace Red as you work with this area of yourself. Red it the colour of passion and action.

Notice how this feels different from last week, how your thought have started change, now fully feel what it is like to have full abundance in your life. To be well, healthy, loved, full of happiness and joy. Fully feel this and experience this wholly. Notice how this feels different from last week, how it feels easier to sense this and then spend some time in gratitude for all you have.

Listen to the Ruby Red Meditation at least once today, twice if you can and fully go into each of the feelings of lack and abundance to fully release your blockages.

Root Chakra Meditation with Mary Magdalene & Ruby Ray Rose

Experience the thoughts and resulting emotions within you that block your abundance in your first root chakra,

See this as a red rose bud. Sit or lay in a comfortable position, your spine straight, erect if sitting, aligned if lying, be relaxed,

Hold the image of a Red Rose Bud in your mind, feel all your resistance to abundance in your life - hold those thoughts that stop you from being fully present eg Life is difficult,

You have to work hard for your money, or Money is the root of all evil.

Hold those thoughts in your mind, feel these fully, they are the blockages within to receiving full abundance
Now open up the Red Rose, image that it holds all you desire, all the things you would like in your life, health, love, happiness, joy, abundance, wealth etc.

See each thought opening up like one of the petals in your hands

Experience them fully with your complete enthusiasm
Recall all your dreams, desires, wishes and all your goals for the future.
Feel this beautiful energy pulsating through your body, aura and being.
Now see the Red Rose transform into a soft pink Rose.

Fill your heart, your mind, your aura, your Root Chakra with this gentle loving energy it may come as a mist to you or within the rose form.

Feel all your gratitude in your heart, mind, soul for all you have in your life, everything you own, personal experiences, friends, loved ones, pets, your home and all you have.

Feel this deeply within and say a few words in your mind of Gratitude for all you have. Feel it with all your complete enthusiasm.

Feel the limitless gratitude with you for everything in your life, your health, your home, your life, love in your life everything

Come back when you are ready
Enjoy your day - beautiful soul

You may wish to keep a journal of what comes up for you on this Blessed Day

Mary Magdalene walks with you each and every day

Day Ten

Sacral Chakra Orange Rose Ray with Mother Mary Meditation

This is the second time you connect to the Sacral Chakra and the Orange rose with Mother Mary. This time you will deeper and each time you revisit the orange rose meditation you will clear old patterns and thoughts.

The orange rose asks you to go deeper again into your relationships, these can be with family, friends and colleagues. Strangers even, for how you interact with others is a key part of your life.

The Sacral Chakra relates to your creativity, it links with the womb or hara area of the body, it is the seat of creation. When this area is balance, mind body and spirit, you are in flow. Being in flow, brings you endless creativity.

This area also relates to how your feel about your sexuality, it is an area that get easily get blocked or out of flow when you are feeling repressed.

As you go deeper again with the sacral chakra and the orange rose, you can release deep beliefs, values, behaviours and emotions.

These will set you free to express more, be in flow and not restrained.

As you connect with your womb space you can connect deeply to Divine Feminime aspects of Mary Magdalene and Kwan Yin as they hold space for you too. Honour your family, friends and guides, ancestors that walk each day with you.

Today we go deeper with your Sacral Chakra and the orange rose ray. You will look at your relationships, with family and friends. Will look at your emotions with relations and other issues in your life. You can explore a little deeper than befoe your own feelings of sexuality.

Hold these feelings, emotions and release with the orange ray. Sit with your womb/hara space and hold your emotions, feel those that sit there within your inner sanctum.

Look back at your life between the years of seven to fourteen, what emotions do you hold from this time in your life.

Connect and hold the emotions, look at the patterns, stories, memories and release them with the meditation. As you connect with your womb space you can connect deeply to Divine Feminime aspects of Mary Magdalene and Kwan Yin as they hold space for you too. Honour

your family, friends and guides, ancestors that walk each day with you.

Love yourself wholly, all aspects of your life and allow

yourself to step through the doorway into the new version of you.

It is time to let go of the old and step into the new Age and its time for you to be you.

Sacral Chakra Orange Rose Ray with Mother Mary Meditation

Go gently inside,

Let all the thoughts of the day slip away

Breathe and go deeply into a gentle slumber

See yourself in a beautiful flower garden and see all the flowers around you they are all orange in colour, so many different flowers but all shades of orange.

You see a water fountain in the garden and by it stands a figure, walk to wards the fountain an you will see it is Mother Mary standing there in blue.

She holds her hands out to greet you and you feel all her love flow towards you.

Stay there holding hands with Mother Mary whilst to revisit in your mind all your thoughts about feeling your true emotions, your true thoughts, times when you felt you couldn't express them, behaviours and values, some may be family values or cultural/religious values allow those thoughts to form into symbolic tears and give them to Mother Mary, she collects them up and puts them into the fountain where they are cleansed and cleared.

Let go of any thoughts of not being enough, any pain or memories from your childhood with your Mother or Father or your own motherhood/fatherhood and any thoughts

about your personal intimacy. Let them flow, give them to Mother Mary and she cleanses them in the fountain.

When you have let everything go, she takes a golden cup and collects some of the water and give you to drink, drink deeply from the cup.

Fully feel all your desires for joy and happiness to be within you, feel all your desires of how you wish your life to be, how you wish your emotions to be

Fully feel everything within you right now,

Mother Mary now gives you an Orange/Coral Rose this means I love you and feel all it energy blend with you, feel it in every cell of your body, every thought is full of love, of joy and feel your true feelings budding within you.

Fully being in this energy of the orange rose as it unfolds within you

Feel gratitude for all the limitless joy and creativity, ways to express yourself unfolding, self confidence to say what you feel

Fully feel all of this with gratitude and happiness

Stay within this energy for as long as you wish

Journal any feelings or visions that come up for you

Rose Journey - Orange Rose Ray with Mother Mary

Describe what did you experience today from the teachings, meditation etc?

Day Eleven

Solar Plexus Chakra with Mary Magdalene and Yellow Rose

Today we connect and explore the realms of yellow and the solar plexus chakra with Magdalene.

The solar plexus is the powerhouse for energy to flow, it is somewhere where if you are bloated you can be holding power, stopping it from flowing freely. The more energy that you can have naturally flowing through the solar plexus the more power and wisdom is yours to tap into.

Lets go deeper into the yellow and into the golden light, to connect to the Solar Sun, the yellow rose and dive into your own powerhouse.

Just be willing to allow this to be released, dissolved, melted away naturally. Get ready to go deep into the solar plexus and connect to your inner wisdom. Into your own gold, into the depths of you. You will notice how you go deeper into your Solar Plexus, into your own emotions and feelings about your own power and wisdom, if you feel any bloating this is advising you to look at your blocks, see where you are playing small, not wanting to stand out and be seen. Where does that emotion or pattern sit within you. Go within and seek it out, is there a word or a phrase that comes to mind eg being seen. You can clear these blocks or fears. You can wear more yellow, eat more yellow foods and consciously draw more gold and yellow into your life.

Listen to your body, your mind and connect to your higher self, ask yourself what is blocking me, go deeper, if you need extra support you can wear something programmed to the Solar Plexus energy eg a pendant or citrine

You can connect more and more to the yellow roses for extra support to release these old patterns.

Mary Magdalene with Yellow Rose Meditation

Sit in a comfortable position or lie down, keeping your spine straight, relax, your whole body and go within, taking some deep breaths, allowing your shoulders to relax and let go of any tension in your body.

Feel the energy of Mary Magdalene draw close, she brings a Yellow colour of energies for you to feel all the healing from this colour.

Call in your guides or helpers too.

Sense yourself within a beautiful garden full of the most amazing flowers you have very seen they are in different colours go and look some of the flowers that are past their blooming phase and take one in your hands.

As you connect to this flower really experience all your thoughts and emotions that block your flow of abundance and feel them flowing into the flower.

Experience the thoughts and resulting emotions that block the flow of abundance in your sacral chakra, all the ways you feel you are powerless or lack the wisdom you need.

Recall in your mind times when you felt fear and any difficulties about expressing your feelings

Feel all your desires in your life with complete enthusiasm fully feeling all your desires to connect with your inner power, your own wisdom, remember times when you were unsure about your abilities your own power and feel each of these emotions.

Play these out in your mind, express how you feel when you cant express yourself fully and how your body feels if you have to bottle up your emotions.

Now Mary Magdalene comes transforms your flower into a beautiful yellow rose and places it next to your heart, feel all the abundance flowing to you, limitless freedom of flowing abundance being poured into you, in the yello rose ray.

Feel it, feel it all, as it blends with you and you can feel where this energy is flowing throughout your body, aura etc.

Now fully feel all the abundance in your life all your wonderful range of emotions that guide you each day, feel the abundance of your own wisdom, your own inner guidance and the ways you express yourself. Feel all your gratitude for everything in your life. Fully feel each petal of the yellow rose and all it brings to you.

Come back when you feel ready

Enjoy your day and write in your journal all you have received.

If anything comes up during the day remember to write about it your journal.

Rose Journey with Mary Magdalene and Yellow Rose

Describe what did you experience today from the teachings, meditation etc?

Day Twelve

Heart Chakra Ruby Rose Ray with Mother Mary

Today we dive into the heart space, open it up, explore the past hurts, set forgiveness into motion and expand your heart chakra. Unity and oneness is the dialogue for ascension, we can not continue to hold more light and love when we hold pain and suffering. So today we delve into the heart space, to release old patterns, programs, old emotions and set yourself free of the old paradigms. It is so liberating, it brings freedom and so much light can pour in. Jesus taught me that so many of these old emotions are about stories we tell ourselves, they are just that, stories or patterns. If there is love there is love. So strip away the hold thought patterns that hold you in the past and open your heart to expansion.

Feel love and hold love in your heart. Explore what love feels like, what do you love? A partner, friend, lover, child, sibling, your environment, what do you love?

Recognise the emotion, the feeling of love? So that you recognise it as it comes to you in its warmth?

Lets go deep today into the heart, in to your heart space, into your inner temple. Lets let go of the old feelings and emotions, lets feel love. Like never before.

Dive into your heart space today.

All that is Love

Go into the meditation with your intention to release all that blocks you from fully loving yourself.

You will be joined by Mother Mary in this meditation she brings her love too.

It's your time to shine, to shine love into your own world and in your whole world. Be the light of the world full of love.

Heart Chakra Ruby Rose Ray Meditation with Mother Mary

Sit in a comfortable position, or lie with your spine straight, relax

Breathe into each breath fully, feeling the air flow into you body into your lungs and feel it as you exhale

Fully feeling each breath, breath by breath relax

Notice anywhere that is in discomfort, direct your breath to that area and relax

fully relax

See yourself on a golden beach with the warm sun, soft sand beneath your feet and the sea waves gently lapping the shore line.

A beautiful sea gull lands by your side and invites you to explore your feelings about unconditional love

As you connect to the sea gull, notice is feathers, its features and see the beauty within the bird

Now notice yourself, your body, your heart, where are you holding on to not allowing love to flow, where do you have resistance to love in your life, what does love feel like, feel it now and see where you have been blocking it out in your life.

Experience fully with your completeness how you do not fully open up to unconditional love, when someone pays you

a compliment how do you react, do you thing no that's not

true, do you accept the compliment?

Fully feel how you are holding back feel this in each breath

Fully own it that you are not fully open to receive love

Now see a figure walking towards you it is Mother Mary she is dressed in blue and white, she brings a small bouncing puppy and it is so alive with desire and love.

As she approaches you feel your heart open wider and wider and when she arrives she holds your hand and guides you to feel all the love of the universe, flowing freely to you, feel this love, follow it , where does it go, where does it end, feel your aura expanding with love wider and wider and wider, where their is only love.

This is your true self a being of love, fulfilled with love

Explore where you let down your control to be loved in a way your thought you should be loved

Play out in your mind incidents when you have compromised yourself to gain approval from another. Feel these emotions rising and let them flow from you.

Mother Mary offers you the loving puppy with all its joy and bountiful energy and you feel its love flow to you, she invites you to let go of all resistance to love and asks you to place all your resistance into a red shell, the moment your old patterns are released to the shell they are transformed into ruby ray roses which Mother Mary gives back to you.

You place these red roses in a hair garland or around your neck, or in what ever way feels right for you.

Now feel all the gratitude for all the loving experiences in your life with your family, friends, pets, loved ones.

Fully feel this love flowing fully thought-out yourself, in each breath there is only love and you fully feel it.

Let your feelings of love and gratitude fully touch everything and everyone you meet today.

Mother Mary holds your hands and your heart cleansing is complete today, she places her hand on your heart with a seal of love.

Spend more time in this blissful place if you wish and visit often.

Journal Everything that comes up for you

Rose Journey Ruby Rose Ray with Mother Mary

Describe what did you experience today from the teachings, meditation etc?

Day Thirteen

Throat Chakra, Blue Rose Ray & Mary Magdalene

Today we connect again with the Blue Ray, with Mary Magdalene's Blue rose. This rose brings the truth of all things, it brings wisdom, healing and love. It helps with communication, to be clear in your words and intention.

Mary wishes you to to use your voice more to speak about what your are feeling.

Dive today deeper into your throat chakra to communicate clearly. Allow your chakra to be a clear channel for your own voice. There will be times in the future when you are called to speak up, and this requires a clear channel for you to communicate. Even with written communication a clear throat chakra allows you to write more concisely and clearer.

Today you will explore your inner blockages within your own communication and explore how you would like to communicate in the future.

Mary Magdalene holds the space for you to explore your own patterns, blockages and helps you to let go and move into the new way of communicating.

If you have an interest in light language or channelling this meditation will help you be an open channel.

Lets explore your own expressions. How do you express yourself, do you write, sing, dance, paint, all these are expressions of your true self.

Meditation with Blue Rose Ray & Mary Magdalene

Sit in a comfortable position, or lie with your spine straight, relax

Breathe into each breath fully, feeling the air flow into you body into your lungs and feel it as you exhale

Fully feeling each breath, breath by breath relax

Notice anywhere that is in discomfort, direct your breath to that area and relax

And fully relax

See a blue mist around you, feel it flowing all around you,

See the mist starting to disperse and as you do so step out into the new landscape, it is fill with blue light, you are in a garden full of blue trees, blue flowers, blue butterflies and walk around the garden exploring everything that is blue, so many shades, hues of blue. Call in Mary Magdalene to join you in this beautiful place.

Before you there is a blue water fountain, see the water flowing in its blue shades of light - Mary invites you to take a drink from the fountain.

Hold your hands under the flowing water, it feels so inviting,

Take a cup and drink from the fountain

Drinking in the blue light, the blue water

Feel it fully in your throat chakra, opening up with the blue water

Sit for a moment fully feeling your resistance to being fully in your truthful light, now you resist to be fully open with others and how you fear rejection and opinions if you speak your truth.

Fully remember when you have said to much and where that emotion sits within you.

Drink again from the fountain and feel your throat chakra area opening up to more and more blue light.

Now fully embrace everything you desire connected to your communications, to fully hear everything, to understand the truth of a situation, to fully be able to express yourself by word, voice, song, written words etc.

Now Mary steps closers and speaks to your Soul, she whispers in her own language the words of love to you.

If you seek to speak light language feel yourself fully being able to do this
Really desire all you wish to be in full abundance, see yourself writing your course, books, poems, artwork, see yourself as the artist, author, poet, speaker

See yourself as you wish to be seen in full abundance it is yours

See the blue light flowing through you with more and more abundance, freeing you from your doubts, from your fears.

Feel all of creation within your throat chakra when communication is fully opened to you.

Now take another drink from the fountain and really

embrace all that you have, give gratitude to your expression, to your confidence, to your vocabulary, to your creativity

Fully be in gratitude in your past, present and future in every communication,
Let the attitude of gratitude touch you when ever you communicate your true feelings during the day

When you feel ready bring yourself back see the blue rose in our hand

Journal everything

Rose Journey Intuition with Blue Rose Ray

Describe what did you experience today from the teachings, meditation etc?

Day Fourteen

Third Eye Intuition with Indigo Moonlight Rose

Today on Day Fourteen we go deeper into the Third Eye, to release any blockages from your Third Eye. To fully open up your intuition, so that you are a clear channel for receiving information in whichever way it comes to you.

We were all born with our own natural intuition, it is our 6th sense, it is connected to the pineal glands and is am important part of being a human being. The more you are in touch with your own intuition the more you can be in touch with your own self.

The third eye allows us to open up more to the massive flow of energy that flows to us every day. It will allow you to be in flow, be it in the office, or work. When we are writing, painting, creating, at all times. It allows us to accesss parts of your past lives, your higher self and soul. By being fully open to receive is a natural process and you can control how much you wish to receive my adjusting your own chakras. You can tune in or tune out whenever you wish. There is no need for protection as such, you only need to say I am open or I am closed. You may have your own phrases but it means the same. It is up to you to be open to receiving or not.

Since intuition is always available the only thing you need to do in order to unlock its potential is to feel your resistance and desire for it and gratefully accept that which is already there within you.

This is your birthright and its is so useful in all aspects of your life.

Dive into your Third Eye.

Be your own Oracle.

You will have read about the different Clairs in Day Six, you can go back and have a quick reminder. The different ways that we receive information. Your own ways that hear, see, feel, know etc.

Note down your own ways that information comes to you, how to do channel it. We are all growing, holding more light, more information etc on a daily basis, just look at how much we scroll by on the internet, we are taking in more and more information day after day. Look at where you are using your discernment, your judgements, about what to read, view, see? Your intuition guides you all the time about what you should or should not read, listen to, see etc.

We need our intuition to be wide open, strong so it can guide us through the barrage of constant flow of information that is being shown to us day after day. Sometimes taking a break from social media or anything online gives us some peace. But this is our way of life now. So we need to be able to navigate it. A strong open third eye helps you to navigate the constant stream of information.

This is the century of information, it flows and flows never stopping and we are in constant flux of it.

So lets go deeper with your Third Eye and the Indigo Rose and my Twin Flame Artun (otherwise know as Solomn - often with me I get a code name and later really know who they are).

Third Eye Intuition Indigo Moon Rose Meditation with Artun Mystic Guide

Sit in a comfortable position, or lie with your spine straight, relax

Breathe into each breath fully, feeling the air flow into you body into your lungs and feel it as you exhale

Fully feeling each breath, breath by breath relax

Notice anywhere that is in discomfort, direct your breath to that area and relax

fully relaxing

Allow yourself to be surrounded by a deep indigo mist and allow it to flow fully to you, see yourself on a small boat, sailing through the mists and you will arrive at small dock area.

As the mists clears step out onto the shoreline.

You at once see you are on a magical beach, on a tropical shoreline, it is dark, you look up and see the full moon, the moon is so bright,

Walk around the shore, feel the sand, pebbles beneath your feet, hear the sound of the water on the shore, hear the sound of fish in the sea,

Fully sense everything - sound, sight, feelings, emotions, hearing everything

What can you hear?
What can you see?
What do you feel?

What emotions do you have?
What do you sense?

This is a place of wonder, a safe beach lit by moon light

You see the outline of a castle on the horizon with interesting turrets and walls, make your way to the castle, you see a figure on the top of the walls, a man dressed in deepest purple you see the colours first in your mind and then in your inner eyes, you know this colour, you see it when the moonlight shines on his robe.

He sends a direct message to you via his telepathy and you sense it straight away, it is a message of hope, of inner knowing and brings you so much joy.

Sense this now.....

You are still making your way to the castle, walking or flying or whatever mode of transport you would like until you reach the castle.

Artun is now before the great castle doors he is waiting for you, he gives you an indigo rose.

When you reach the doors he greets you and invites you to go inside the castle, you are guided through the great hall, chambers and up to the top of the castle and invited to look out at the full moon, to the stars,

Artun shows you the stars in the sky, he points out different constellations to you,

He shows how they line up ready for changes in our earthly world

He asks you to let go of all your resistance to fully believing in

the intuition that comes to you, to let go of all your fears that hold you back from being fully open in your intuition.

He gives you time to fully remember when you wished you had used your intuition in the past and any emotions that are attached to this.

He says pour all these thoughts, memories, fears into a cup that he holds out for you, and you see each be received in the form of small daisies, each memory is a daisy, each fear a daisy and you fill up the cup with your daisies.

When you have fully released all your fears and thoughts into many daisies, Artun throws them up into the sky and they are transformed into star dust and he give you a cup of star dust, These are so full of potential.

Now think about every desire you have to be fully abundant, how much you want your inner knowing to expand, how you would like your intuition to grow and for you to fully trust all your receive.

Consider the ways you might like your inner wisdom to come to you, do you wish to hear more, feel more, know more.

Feel an abundance of inner knowing within you, for it is fully within you

If you wish to receive more messages from light beings, feel that now, if you wish to receive a stronger connection to

Mary Magdalene to Jesus, to God, to the Angels or Divine Councils feel that now as if you have a hot line to them. Feel their love and messages flow directly to you now.

If you wish to speak with light language or connect more to the Lemurians, Arcturians, Sirians, Pleiadians, Dragons etc

Ask for this now and fully feel the energies of connecting to them.

Spend a few minutes with Artun he can show you how to connect to different dimensions, different vibrations of energies etc.

Ask to be shown how to receive inner knowing and intuition from your higher self, from your Soul and he will show you and deepen that connection.

When you feel ready leave the castle

Thank Artun for his teachings, for his wisdom, knowledge and for sharing his indigo rose and other gifts with you.

Fully feel all your gratitude for everything you have received and for everything you have in your life.

Gratitude for your inner knowing

Feel your gratitude for all your past, present and future experiences

When you feel ready return to the here and now

Enjoy your day

Journal everything for there is meaning in your meditations.

Rose Journey Intuition with Indigo Moon with Artun Mystic Guide

Describe what did you experience today from the teachings, meditation etc?

Day Fifteen

Crown Chakra, Divine I AM energy with Mary Magdalene & Council of Light - Open up to your True Self - White Rose

Today we revisit your Crown chakra with Mary Magdalene and the I AM energy and the white rose. Connecting to your own enlightment. Your own unique connection to the Divine, to the Universe and all that is, an more. To the Pledians, Galactics to the Councils of light.

To clear and open your crown chakra wider and wider to embody more and more light.

You are the Divine I AM energy
You are connected to all things
All things You Are

Nothing much can be said about enlightenment – even Buddha is silent about it, he smiled when asked and showed a flower.

I give you a Rose Flower or a Lotus Flower as a symbol of enlightenment, its the pure state where the ego dissolves and you realise you are the All that is, you are the Divine of the Universe, the Universe resides in you.

You are stardust.

I connect Mary Magdalene, Jesus, Goddess Isis and many others in the Council of Light, a collective consciousness of beings who send us teachings, messages and wisdom as we open up our crown chakras to receive more from the universe, cosmos.

One of their clear messages is one of Being, just to be, at peace, calm, with peace of mind within the awaken state of pure being, pure Bliss.

If you have no thoughts or wanting anything you are in this perfect state of just being.

At Peace with everything. Anandmayi Ma spoke often about this sense of pure Joy being.

Knowing yourself being at peace with yourself being at one with everything and yourself.

Lets return again to the thoughts or no thoughts of just being, at one with everything. Just breathing and being still in that pure I AM energy.

Being your true self in this perfect moment, moment by moment in perfect stillness and peace.

We are each unique divine beings and when you fully connect to your crown chakra you fully feel this. It is hard to explain enlightment it can be like the Buddha says being silent just doing nothing, being no-thing, this is enlightment, when we stop trying to do things, we are just be-ing our divine selves.

We are likened to the lotus flower or the rose, we are beauty itself and we know that this is what we are.

When we have dropped the soul searching for finding ourselves, finding our purpose, finding what makes us happy, we find it there in ourselves it was there all along, we dont need the fancy job, the new car, the purpose, at our core, our true self we are enlighted in just being.

We feel this in meditation, this sense of joy in being in the now.

Finding this perfect state of being can be by being in the heart, being in our own essence, our zero point, perfect balance and there is one thing that more of us have experience this year is time.

We have had more time to be, just be and this helps us on our ascension path, to be at peace. That's when you shut off the fear of a virus, fear of a vaccine, fear of death, illness etc.

We each have our own triggers around our fears and you may have found that you have different opinions to others, this is all part of the same truth, the different ways we perceive our lives, our different experiences from different perspectives.

Do not get involved with arguments or disagreements about different opinions as the truth can be different through different eyes.

Stepping into no judgements of others is part of the ascension, stepping away from the dramas. The old ways of 3D patterns playing out that divide us as humans.

So we are seeking to let go of our resistance to Just BE, letting go of our difficulty in switching the world out, getting off the rollercoaster of making a living and start being in our lives, connecting deeply to ourselves as our true self.

We are going to explore releasing all fears of connecting to the Divine Source of all things and fully experience Joy and happiness in all things.

Connecting to balance, calm, peace and the awaken state of pure bliss.

We have two ascended masters as guides with this meditation we have Mary Magdalene and Anandmayi Ma with the white rose.

You will go on a journey to the Delphi Temple to meet with the Priestesses and Priests of the white rose garden and receive a light transmission.

Be in peace

I AM Joy

I AM Bliss

Crown Chakra, Divine I AM energy with Mary Magdalene & Anandmayi Ma Meditation - White Rose

This meditation was channelled to be received with the white rose, in a white Rose Garden with you Mary Magdalene and Anandmayi Ma these two pure essences of love and light wish to bring you a light transmission with the energies of the white rose. To open your crown up to unlimited divinity.

Make yourself comfortable and relax, closing your eyes and going within.

Take some deep breaths and relax

Relax now

Feel yourself becoming more and more relaxed

See yourself surrounded by a white mist, it is so bright and you feel the urge to go deeper into your relaxation, do so now

Fee the white surround you and embrace you and count to 5

1, 2 3 4 5 going deeper and deeper into the white

As the mist clears you see yourself before a greek temple with pillars, before the temple is a garden full of roses, you notice that they are all white, different types of roses, all white, small ones, double ones, all pure white.

As you marvel at the roses, you notice priestesses and priests come to join you, they are dressed in white too.

They guide you into the temple and give you a white rose and garland of white roses which you can either have on your head or around your neck.

As you go into the temple you see figures before the altar, you look down, the floor is white marble and it feels so smooth beneath your feet, the altar is made of white marble too. Notice everything on the altar, the candles the white roses adorn it and see everything else that is there.

The two figures step forward you feel Mary Magdalene's essence straight away, she lifts a veil and shows herself in her true beauty, she feels so powerful, more powerful than you may have experienced before - connect with her energy now and fully feel her energy ....

Anandamayi Ma now steps forward and greets you, smiling, you feel waves of excitement meeting her in this sacred temple. Connect deeply to her too.....

They invite you to stand on a circular area within the temple, you look up and see a shaft of light that flows into the temple.

They draw down the white light and direct it to your crown.

Feel it flowing to you, a light beam of white pure light

It comes in waves of light, beaming down on you

This is a direct light beam of light from Source to you.

Stay in the temple as long as you like

You have received Divine Light and you will notice how your crown connection has widen and opened you up more and more to divine light.

Look around you and see beings of light from the Divine Council of Light they are overseeing everything.

Each time you connect with this meditation you will receive more and more divine light.

And so it is

Bring yourself back

Record in your Journal

Blessed Be

Rose Journey Crown Chakra, Divine I AM energy with Mary Magdalene & Anandmayi Ma - White rose

Describe what did you experience today from the teachings, meditation etc?

Day Sixteen

Mary Magdalene's Pink Bliss & Ruby Red Rose

Now on day Sixteen we go deeper again once more, we connect with the Mary Magdalene's Pink Bliss light and the Root Chakra Ruby Red energies. You have two meditations today to start the last seven days of this course.

You will notice changes in what comes up for you, the course has been designed just this way. So that you look at blockages each week and release your resistance to abundance, happiness, joy, health and wealth over the three weeks.

This course is intensive, but it need only take up twenty to thirty minutes a day to be effective, consistency is the key. To make daily changes to your life.

As you go deeper with each of the three weeks you really go deeper into releasing old thought patterns, old programming and outdated ways of living to fully delve into the limitless possibilities of life.

You will notice different things coming up for you to release and let go off relating to each of the chakras and their corresponding emotions.

By continuing with the course for the full 22 days you will really embody the healing energies of each flower and its colour with the continuing support of Mary Magdalene.

During the past week you will have noticed changes within your thinking patterns, shifts of resistance starting to move and new ways of thinking about your life and yourself.

When you go through each of the meditations during this week you will notice how the energy feels deeper this time.

Remember to journal everything down and look deeper at everything that comes up for you.

So lets really got deep with the Pink Bliss holding space for you and the Ruby Red energies with Mary Magdalene showing you the way to let go, move forward, be whole in peace and harmony.

If you listen to the Pink Bliss to set intentions for the next stage it will hold you, support you and guide you forward.

Allow Mary Magdalene and her pink roses to come to you and feel her energy envelope you with her love.
The Pink Bliss rose and its loving energy of self love links to your higher heart chakra which sits on your Thymus above your heart below your throat area. It is the area that connects you deeply to your higher self and to your divine self. An area of deep self love.

The intentions for this pink rose are:

I love and accept myself just as I am.
I allow myself to unfold like a rose each
and every day, living in love.

You will really feel the shift in your energies between the White Rose of Day Eight and moving back to the Ruby Red Rose of the Root Chakra, it will be like coming home to yourself a comfortable feeling and it will ground you after you have been working with the upper chakras.

So we return to your core, to money, to struggles and you will experience them again and release them. Experience your thoughts to do with abundance and lack in your life.

The energy of the root chakra is:

Living in complete Abundance
Living in love, happiness, wealth and health

Diving into all that Abundance
Means to you

Meditation with Pink Bliss & Mary Magdalene

Go into yourself, breathe, go within, step beneath the veil inside

Surround yourself with Pink Mist Light
Allow it to flow around your feet,
Your ankles, knees, your thighs
Your body, root chakra, up to your sacral chakra
Up to your Solar Plexus and on to your heart
Pause there and see a pink rose forming
Step into your Pink Rose
Be at one with your Pink Rose
Feel the petals
The softness of the Petals
You are the beautiful Pink Rose
Feel all the peace and bliss from the pink rose within you
Spend some time in this beautiful soothing, supporting energy of Self Love

Feel the presences of Mary Magdalene join you
First you sense her heavenly perfume coming towards you
Then you see her with your spiritual eyes
Then you feel the touch of her gentle hands
Holding yours for sometime

Blessings flow from her to you
She gives you a Key a Golden Ankh
This is the Key to unlock your endless Joy and Abundant Heart

Breathe deeply and deeply going into the Pink Bliss energy
Going deeper and deeper into the Pink Mist

See yourself surrounded by the Pink Bliss
Feel it melt away all your fears, worries, anxiety
Feel the pink bliss loving energy surround you
Fully be the Bliss energy
You are the Bliss energy it is you

Spend some time in this energy

Come back when you feel ready

You are ready to begin this journey into your heart

Connect to the Ruby Red Meditation on this day too as you begin another week with Mary Magdalene and Mother Mary holding sacred space for you.

Root Chakra Meditation with Mary Magdalene & Ruby Ray Rose

Experience the thoughts and resulting emotions within you that block your abundance in your first root chakra,

See this as a red rose bud. Sit or lay in a comfortable position, your spine straight, erect if sitting, aligned if lying, be relaxed,

Hold the image of a Red Rose Bud in your mind, feel all your resistance to abundance in your life - hold those thoughts that stop you from being fully present eg Life is difficult,

You have to work hard for your money, or Money is the root of all evil.

Hold those thoughts in your mind, feel these fully, they are the blockages within to receiving full abundance
Now open up the Red Rose, image that it holds all you desire, all the things you would like in your life, health, love, happiness, joy, abundance, wealth etc.

See each thought opening up like one of the petals in your hands

Experience them fully with your complete enthusiasm
Recall all your dreams, desires, wishes and all your goals for the future.
Feel this beautiful energy pulsating through your body, aura and being.
Now see the Red Rose transform into a soft pink Rose.

Fill your heart, your mind, your aura, your Root Chakra with this gentle loving energy it may come as a mist to you or within the rose form.

Feel all your gratitude in your heart, mind, soul for all you have in your life, everything you own, personal experiences, friends, loved ones, pets, your home and all you have.

Feel this deeply within and say a few words in your mind of Gratitude for all you have. Feel it with all your complete enthusiasm.

Feel the limitless gratitude with you for everything in your life, your health, your home, your life, love in your life everything

Come back when you are ready
Enjoy your day - beautiful soul

You may wish to keep a journal of what comes up for you on this Blessed Day

Mary Magdalene walks with you each and every day

Rose Journey Pink Bliss Rose & Ruby Red

Describe what did you experience today from the teachings, meditation etc?

Day Seventeen

Sacral Chakra Orange Rose Ray with Mother Mary Meditation

Today on Day Seventeen we revisit the Sacral Chakra, the seat of relationships, you will be supported by an orange rose and Mother Mary.

This time you will deeper and each time you revisit the orange rose meditation you will clear old patterns and thoughts.

The orange rose asks you to go deeper again into your relationships, these can be with family, friends and colleagues.

Strangers even, for how you interact with others is a key part of your life. How do you react with others outside of your family, are you confident? Are you shy? I used to be mega confident, but over the years it has dwindled so this is one of my areas for improvement. After the "stay at home" message you might be nervous about meeting others, been used to a small circle of friends. Now is the time to "shine your light" and you can do this by meeting more people again.

The Sacral Chakra relates to your creativity, it links with the womb or hara area of the body, it is the seat of creation.

When this area is balance, mind body and spirit, you are in flow. Being in flow, brings you endless creativity.

This area also relates to how your feel about your sexuality, it is an area that get easily get blocked or out of flow when you are feeling repressed.

As you go deeper again with the sacral chakra and the orange rose, you can release deep beliefs, values, behaviours and emotions.

These will set you free to express more, be in flow and not restrained.

As you connect with your womb space you can connect deeply to Divine Feminime aspects of Mary Magdalene and Kwan Yin as they hold space for you too.

Honour your family, friends and guides, ancestors that walk each day with you The veil is very thin now and many mediums and channellers have mentioned that it is barely there now, as you raise your vibration the veil becomes more and more visible, the voices are clearer too.

Today we go deeper with your Sacral Chakra and the orange rose ray. You will look at your relationships, with family and friends. Will look at your emotions with relations and other issues in your life. You can explore a little deeper than befoe your own feelings of sexuality.

Hold these feelings, emotions and release with the orange ray. Sit with your womb/hara space and hold your emotions, feel those that sit there within your inner sanctum.

Look back at your life between the years of seven to fourteen, what emotions do you hold from this time in your life.

Connect and hold the emotions, look at the patterns, stories, memories and release them with the meditation. As you connect with your womb space you can connect deeply to Divine Feminime aspects of Mary Magdalene and Kwan Yin as they hold space for you too.

Sacral Chakra Orange Rose Ray with Mother Mary Meditation

Go gently inside,

Let all the thoughts of the day slip away

Breathe and go deeply into a gentle slumber

See yourself in a beautiful flower garden and see all the flowers around you they are all orange in colour, so many different flowers but all shades of orange.

You see a water fountain in the garden and by it stands a figure, walk to wards the fountain an you will see it is Mother Mary standing there in blue.

She holds her hands out to greet you and you feel all her love flow towards you.

Stay there holding hands with Mother Mary whilst to revisit in your mind all your thoughts about feeling your true emotions, your true thoughts, times when you felt you couldn't express them, behaviours and values, some may be family values or cultural/religious values allow those thoughts to form into symbolic tears and give them to Mother Mary, she collects them up and puts them into the fountain where they are cleansed and cleared.

Let go of any thoughts of not being enough, any pain or memories from your childhood with your Mother or Father or your own motherhood/fatherhood and any thoughts

about your personal intimacy. Let them flow, give them to Mother Mary and she cleanses them in the fountain.

When you have let everything go, she takes a golden cup and collects some of the water and give you to drink, drink deeply from the cup.

Fully feel all your desires for joy and happiness to be within you, feel all your desires of how you wish your life to be, how you wish your emotions to be

Fully feel everything within you right now,

Mother Mary now gives you an Orange/Coral Rose this means I love you and feel all it energy blend with you, feel it in every cell of your body, every thought is full of love, of joy and feel your true feelings budding within you.

Fully being in this energy of the orange rose as it unfolds within you

Feel gratitude for all the limitless joy and creativity, ways to express yourself unfolding, self confidence to say what you feel

Fully feel all of this with gratitude and happiness

Stay within this energy for as long as you wish

Journal any feelings or visions that come up for you

Rose Journey - Orange Rose Ray with Mother Mary

Describe what did you experience today from the teachings, meditation etc?

Day Eighteen

Solar Plexus Chakra with Mary Magdalene and Yellow Rose

Today we reconnect and explore the realms of yellow and the solar plexus chakra with Magdalene. This will be your second time of connecting to your solar plexus to release more from your powerhouse of energy.

Lets go deeper into the yellow and into the golden light, to connect to the Solar Sun, the yellow rose and dive into your own powerhouse.

Just be willing to allow this to be released, dissolved, melted away naturally.

Get ready to go deep into the solar plexus and connect to your inner wisdom. Into your own gold, into the depths of you. You will notice how you go deeper into your Solar Plexus, into your own emotions and feelings about your own power and wisdom, if you feel any bloating this is advising you to look at your blocks, see where you are playing small, not wanting to stand out and be seen. Where does that emotion or pattern sit within you.

Go within and seek it out, is there a word or a phrase that comes to mind eg being seen. You can clear these blocks or fears.

You can wear more yellow, eat more yellow foods and consciously draw more gold and yellow into your life.

Listen to your body, your mind and connect to your higher self, ask yourself what is blocking me, go deeper, if you need extra support you can wear something programmed to the Solar Plexus energy eg a pendant or citrine.

You can connect more and more to the yellow roses for extra support to release these old patterns.

Mary Magdalene with Yellow Rose Meditation

Sit in a comfortable position or lie down, keeping your spine straight, relax, your whole body and go within, taking some deep breaths, allowing your shoulders to relax and let go of any tension in your body.

Feel the energy of Mary Magdalene draw close, she brings a Yellow colour of energies for you to feel all the healing from this colour.

Call in your guides or helpers too.

Sense yourself within a beautiful garden full of the most amazing flowers you have very seen they are in different colours go and look some of the flowers that are past their blooming phase and take one in your hands.

As you connect to this flower really experience all your thoughts and emotions that block your flow of abundance and feel them flowing into the flower.

Experience the thoughts and resulting emotions that block the flow of abundance in your sacral chakra, all the ways you feel you are powerless or lack the wisdom you need.

Recall in your mind times when you felt fear and any difficulties about expressing your feelings

Feel all your desires in your life with complete enthusiasm fully feeling all your desires to connect with your inner power, your own wisdom, remember times when you were unsure about your abilities your own power and feel each of these emotions.

Play these out in your mind, express how you feel when you cant express yourself fully and how your body feels if you have to bottle up your emotions.

Now Mary Magdalene comes transforms your flower into a beautiful yellow rose and places it next to your heart, feel all the abundance flowing to you, limitless freedom of flowing abundance being poured into you, in the yello rose ray.

Feel it, feel it all, as it blends with you and you can feel where this energy is flowing throughout your body, aura etc.

Now fully feel all the abundance in your life all your wonderful range of emotions that guide you each day, feel the abundance of your own wisdom, your own inner guidance and the ways you express yourself. Feel all your gratitude for everything in your life. Fully feel each petal of the yellow rose and all it brings to you.

Come back when you feel ready

Enjoy your day and write in your journal all you have received.

If anything comes up during the day remember to write about it your journal.

Rose Journey with Mary Magdalene and Yellow Rose

Describe what did you experience today from the teachings, meditation etc?

Day Nineteen

Heart Chakra Ruby Rose Ray with Mother Mary

On Day Nineteen we visit the heart again, to open it up, explore any past hurts that remain. Forgive ourself and others and open up to receiving more love. So you can share more love with others.

So lets go deeper into the heart space, into your own heart, to clear out any blockages, anything holding you back from love.

So today we delve into the heart space, to release old patterns, programs, old emotions and set yourself free of the old paradigms.

It is so liberating, it brings freedom and so much light can pour in.

Remember our life is just a stories, we are Soul having a human experience, we are eternal.

Feel love and hold love in your heart. Explore what love feels like, what do you love? A partner, friend, lover, child, sibling, your environment, what do you love?

Recognise the emotion, the feeling of love? So that you recognise it as it comes to you in its warmth?

Lets go deep today into the heart, in to your heart space, into your inner temple.

Lets let go of the old feelings and emotions, lets feel love. Like never before.

Dive into your heart space today.

All that is Love

Go into the meditation with your intention to release all that blocks you from fully loving yourself.

You will be joined by Mother Mary in this meditation she brings her love too.

It's your time to shine, to shine love into your own world and in your whole world.

Be the light of the world full of love.

Heart Chakra Ruby Rose Ray
Meditation with Mother Mary

Sit in a comfortable position, or lie with your spine straight, relax

Breathe into each breath fully, feeling the air flow into you body into your lungs and feel it as you exhale

Fully feeling each breath, breath by breath relax

Notice anywhere that is in discomfort, direct your breath to that area and relax

fully relax

See yourself on a golden beach with the warm sun, soft sand beneath your feet and the sea waves gently lapping the shore line.

A beautiful sea gull lands by your side and invites you to explore your feelings about unconditional love

As you connect to the sea gull, notice is feathers, its features and see the beauty within the bird

Now notice yourself, your body, your heart, where are you holding on to not allowing love to flow, where do you have resistance to love in your life, what does love feel like, feel it now and see where you have been blocking it out in your life.

Experience fully with your completeness how you do not fully open up to unconditional love, when someone pays you

a compliment how do you react, do you thing no that's not true, do you accept the compliment?

Fully feel how you are holding back feel this in each breath

Fully own it that you are not fully open to receive love

Now see a figure walking towards you it is Mother Mary she is dressed in blue and white, she brings a small bouncing puppy and it is so alive with desire and love.

As she approaches you feel your heart open wider and wider and when she arrives she holds your hand and guides you to feel all the love of the universe, flowing freely to you, feel this love, follow it , where does it go, where does it end, feel your aura expanding with love wider and wider and wider, where their is only love.

This is your true self a being of love, fulfilled with love

Explore where you let down your control to be loved in a way your thought you should be loved

Play out in your mind incidents when you have compromised yourself to gain approval from another. Feel these emotions rising and let them flow from you.

Mother Mary offers you the loving puppy with all its joy and bountiful energy and you feel its love flow to you, she invites you to let go of all resistance to love and asks you to place all your resistance into a red shell, the moment your old patterns are released to the shell they are transformed into ruby ray roses which Mother Mary gives back to you.

You place these red roses in a hair garland or around your neck, or in what ever way feels right for you.

Now feel all the gratitude for all the loving experiences in your life with your family, friends, pets, loved ones.

Fully feel this love flowing fully thought-out yourself, in each breath there is only love and you fully feel it.

Let your feelings of love and gratitude fully touch everything and everyone you meet today.

Mother Mary holds your hands and your heart cleansing is complete today, she places her hand on your heart with a seal of love.

Spend more time in this blissful place if you wish and visit often.

Journal Everything that comes up for you

Rose Journey Ruby Rose Ray with Mother Mary

Describe what did you experience today from the teachings, meditation etc?

Day Twenty

Throat Chakra, Blue Rose Ray & Mary Magdalene

This is the last time you will visit the Throat chakras with the blue rose ray and Mary Magdalene.

The blue rose is often associated with Mary Magdalene as are the other colours of pink, white and red. But in particular the blue rose of truth and inner wisdom is one that sets you free.

As you learn more about yourself and Mary Magdalene's life, whereas she wasn't what we were told in the Bible, she was a healer, mystic and important part of the early Christian church and more more truths are coming to light.

In your life you as you connect to clear and express yourself more, you will be bringing your own truths to light too.

You may write or paint, or other expressions of yourself and in everything you do, you will share the depths of your own self.

Mary wishes you to to use your voice more to speak about what your are feeling. She wishes you to create, to be seen, heard and your words and expressions are needed in the world today.

Dive today deeper into your throat chakra to communicate clearly.

Allow your chakra to be a clear channel for your own voice.

There will be times in the future when you are called to speak up, and this requires a clear channel for you to communicate.

Today you will explore your inner blockages within your own communication and explore how you would like to communicate in the future.

Mary Magdalene holds the space for you to explore your own patterns, blockages and helps you to let go and move into the new way of communicating.

Meditation with Blue Rose Ray & Mary Magdalene

Sit in a comfortable position, or lie with your spine straight, relax

Breathe into each breath fully, feeling the air flow into you body into your lungs and feel it as you exhale

Fully feeling each breath, breath by breath relax

Notice anywhere that is in discomfort, direct your breath to that area and relax

And fully relax

See a blue mist around you, feel it flowing all around you,

See the mist starting to disperse and as you do so step out into the new landscape, it is fill with blue light, you are in a garden full of blue trees, blue flowers, blue butterflies and walk around the garden exploring everything that is blue, so many shades, hues of blue. Call in Mary Magdalene to join you in this beautiful place.

Before you there is a blue water fountain, see the water flowing in its blue shades of light - Mary invites you to take a drink from the fountain.

Hold your hands under the flowing water, it feels so inviting,

Take a cup and drink from the fountain

Drinking in the blue light, the blue water

Feel it fully in your throat chakra, opening up with the blue water

Sit for a moment fully feeling your resistance to being fully in your truthful light, now you resist to be fully open with others *and how you fear rejection and opinions if you speak your truth.*

Fully remember when you have said to much and where that emotion sits within you.

Drink again from the fountain and feel your throat chakra area opening up to more and more blue light.

Now fully embrace everything you desire connected to your communications, to fully hear everything, to understand the truth of a situation, to fully be able to express yourself by word, voice, song, written words etc.

Now Mary steps closers and speaks to your Soul, she whispers in her own language the words of love to you.

If you seek to speak light language feel yourself fully being able to do this
Really desire all you wish to be in full abundance, see yourself writing your course, books, poems, artwork, see yourself as the artist, author, poet, speaker

See yourself as you wish to be seen in full abundance it is yours

See the blue light flowing through you with more and more abundance, freeing you from your doubts, from your fears.

Feel all of creation within your throat chakra when communication is fully opened to you.

Now take another drink from the fountain and really embrace all that you have, give gratitude to your expression, to your confidence, to your vocabulary, to your creativity

Fully be in gratitude in your past, present and future in every communication,
Let the attitude of gratitude touch you when ever you communicate your true feelings during the day

When you feel ready bring yourself back see the blue rose in our hand

Journal everything

Rose Journey Intuition with Blue Rose Ray

Describe what did you experience today from the teachings, meditation etc?

Day Twenty One

Third Eye Intuition with Indigo Moonlight Rose

Today on Day Twenty One and this is the last day to clear and open up your intuition, with your third eye. If you wish to explore your Intuition more, I shall be writing a book on Awareness later in 2022 so watch for that on my Author Page on Amazon. Earlier this year I ran a course on this using different techniques and I have taught awareness classes for many years.

Sixth sense is something we all have, we felt this as children and learnt to close it down, as in this lifetime it wasn't needed or part of our society. Now we are opening it up again, it is time to be fully open to receive the messages all around us. The more you are in touch with your own intuition the more you can be in touch with your own self.

Explore your own intuition again, look at your strengths, you can set intentions today for clearer communication, different ways to receive information eg you can ask for more images, clearer understanding about what things mean. I personally see things eg a bucket, just the other

Since intuition is always available the only thing you need to do in order to unlock its potential is to feel your resistance and desire for it and gratefully accept that which is already there within you.

This is your birthright and its is so useful in all aspects of your life.

Dive into your Third Eye.

Be your own Oracle.

You will have read about the different Clairs in Day Six, you can go back and have a quick reminder. The different ways that we receive information. Your own ways that hear, see, feel, know etc.

We need our intuition to be wide open, strong so it can guide us through the barrage of constant flow of information that is being shown to us day after day.

Lets go deeper into your Third Eye with Artun Mystic Guide today.

Third Eye Intuition Indigo Moon Rose Meditation with Artun Mystic Guide

Sit in a comfortable position, or lie with your spine straight, relax
Breathe into each breath fully, feeling the air flow into you body into your lungs and feel it as you exhale

Fully feeling each breath, breath by breath relax

Notice anywhere that is in discomfort, direct your breath to that area and relax

fully relaxing

Allow yourself to be surrounded by a deep indigo mist and allow it to flow fully to you, see yourself on a small boat, sailing through the mists and you will arrive at small dock area.

As the mists clears step out onto the shoreline.

You at once see you are on a magical beach, on a tropical shoreline, it is dark, you look up and see the full moon, the moon is so bright,

Walk around the shore, feel the sand, pebbles beneath your feet, hear the sound of the water on the shore, hear the sound of fish in the sea,

Fully sense everything - sound, sight, feelings, emotions, hearing everything

What can you hear?
What can you see?
What do you feel?

What emotions do you have?
What do you sense?

This is a place of wonder, a safe beach lit by moon light

You see the outline of a castle on the horizon with interesting turrets and walls, make your way to the castle, you see a figure on the top of the walls, a man dressed in deepest purple you see the colours first in your mind and then in your inner eyes, you know this colour, you see it when the moonlight shines on his robe.

He sends a direct message to you via his telepathy and you sense it straight away, it is a message of hope, of inner knowing and brings you so much joy.

Sense this now.....

You are still making your way to the castle, walking or flying or whatever mode of transport you would like until you reach the castle.

Artun is now before the great castle doors he is waiting for you, he gives you an indigo rose.

When you reach the doors he greets you and invites you to go inside the castle, you are guided through the great hall, chambers and up to the top of the castle and invited to look out at the full moon, to the stars,

Artun shows you the stars in the sky, he points out different constellations to you,

He shows how they line up ready for changes in our earthly world

He asks you to let go of all your resistance to fully believing in

the intuition that comes to you, to let go of all your fears that hold you back from being fully open in your intuition.

He gives you time to fully remember when you wished you had used your intuition in the past and any emotions that are attached to this.

He says pour all these thoughts, memories, fears into a cup that he holds out for you, and you see each be received in the form of small daisies, each memory is a daisy, each fear a daisy and you fill up the cup with your daisies.

When you have fully released all your fears and thoughts into many daisies, Artun throws them up into the sky and they are transformed into star dust and he give you a cup of star dust, These are so full of potential.

Now think about every desire you have to be fully abundant, how much you want your inner knowing to expand, how you would like your intuition to grow and for you to fully trust all your receive.

Consider the ways you might like your inner wisdom to come to you, do you wish to hear more, feel more, know more.

Feel an abundance of inner knowing within you, for it is fully within you

If you wish to receive more messages from light beings, feel that now, if you wish to receive a stronger connection to Mary Magdalene to Jesus, to God, to the Angels or Divine Councils feel that now as if you have a hot line to them. Feel their love and messages flow directly to you now.

If you wish to speak with light language or connect more to the Lemurians, Arcturians, Sirians, Pleidians, Dragons etc Ask for this now and fully feel the energies of connecting to them.

Spend a few minutes with Artun he can show you how to connect to different dimensions, different vibrations of energies etc.

Ask to be shown how to receive inner knowing and intuition from your higher self, from your Soul and he will show you and deepen that connection.

When you feel ready leave the castle

Thank Artun for his teachings, for his wisdom, knowledge and for sharing his indigo rose and other gifts with you.

Fully feel all your gratitude for everything you have received and for everything you have in your life.

Gratitude for your inner knowing

Feel your gratitude for all your past, present and future experiences

When you feel ready return to the here and now

Enjoy your day

Journal everything for there is meaning in your meditations.

Rose Journey Intuition with Indigo Moon with Artun Mystic Guide

Describe what did you experience today from the teachings, meditation etc?

Day Twenty Two

Crown Chakra, Divine I AM energy with Mary Magdalene & Council of Light - Open up to your True Self - White Rose

Today we revisit your Crown chakra with Mary Magdalene and the I AM energy and the white rose for the last time in this course. You can however, relisten to the meditations at any time you wish. I complete this whole 22 days every year myself, usually in September as this is time that calls to me to clear and renew my own body, mind and intentions. So you may wish to do this too.

You are the Divine I AM energy
You are connected to all things
All things You Are

So how are you feeling on this last day of the 22 days course, today is a good day to start your own reflections, looking back over the course and seeing where you have released emotions, patterns, thought patterns etc.

Today fully connect to your own I AM energy, you are connected to the whole universe, part of everything.

Mary Magdalene wishes to thank you for joining her and Mother Mary on this course, she brings her love to you today and everyday.

Do something special today on this last day, have a treat, walk in nature, gift yourself some flowers, oils, have a pamper or meal.

Embrace how far you have come in this week its a journey from day one to now day twenty two. A powerful releasing time and honouring yourself and how far you have come.

Well Done for getting this far.

One last meditation connecting to the I AM energy, with the white rose and Mary Magdalane with Anandmayi Ma today. Bring in the Bliss enlightment energy, really feel at one with everything. Feel the joy of everything in your life. Feel the happiness in any given moment, and the love within your heart.

Connect to the White Rose today you wish to bring in a White Lotus flower too.

Lets return again to the thoughts or no thoughts of just being, at one with everything. Just breathing and being still in that pure I AM energy.

Crown Chakra, Divine I AM energy with Mary Magdalene & Anandmayi Ma Meditation - White Rose

This meditation was channelled to be received with the white rose, in a white Rose Garden with you Mary Magdalene and Anandmayi Ma these two pure essences of love and light wish to bring you a light transmission with the energies of the white rose. To open your crown up to unlimited divinity.

Make yourself comfortable and relax, closing your eyes and going within.

Take some deep breaths and relax

Relax now

Feel yourself becoming more and more relaxed

See yourself surrounded by a white mist, it is so bright and you feel the urge to go deeper into your relaxation, do so now

Fee the white surround you and embrace you and count to 5

1, 2 3 4 5 going deeper and deeper into the white

As the mist clears you see yourself before a greek temple with pillars, before the temple is a garden full of roses, you notice that they are all white, different types of roses, all white, small ones, double ones, all pure white.

As you marvel at the roses, you notice priestesses and priests come to join you, they are dressed in white too.

They guide you into the temple and give you a white rose and garland of white roses which you can either have on your head or around your neck.

As you go into the temple you see figures before the altar, you look down, the floor is white marble and it feels so smooth beneath your feet, the altar is made of white marble too. Notice everything on the altar, the candles the white roses adorn it and see everything else that is there.

The two figures step forward you feel Mary Magdalene's essence straight away, she lifts a veil and shows herself in her true beauty, she feels so powerful, more powerful than you may have experienced before - connect with her energy now and fully feel her energy ....

Anandamayi Ma now steps forward and greets you, smiling, you feel waves of excitement meeting her in this sacred temple. Connect deeply to her too.....

They invite you to stand on a circular area within the temple, you look up and see a shaft of light that flows into the temple.

They draw down the white light and direct it to your crown.

Feel it flowing to you, a light beam of white pure light

It comes in waves of light, beaming down on you

This is a direct light beam of light from Source to you.

Stay in the temple as long as you like

You have received Divine Light and you will notice how your crown connection has widen and opened you up more and more to divine light.

Look around you and see beings of light from the Divine Council of Light they are overseeing everything.

Each time you connect with this meditation you will receive more and more divine light.

And so it is

Bring yourself back

Record in your Journal

Blessed Be

If you have enjoyed this course you may be interested in my White Flame teachings, they come with the symbols of the White Rose, White Ankh, White Lotus flower and initiations and attunements to White Flame energies.

Sacred Temple of the White Flame by Kim Ora Rose

Rose Journey Crown Chakra, Divine I AM energy with Mary Magdalene & Anandmayi Ma - White rose

Describe what did you experience today from the teachings, meditation etc?

A Note from the Author

Thank you for buying this book the 22 day course started as an online course and this year I decided to formally rewrite the daily activities and meditation scripts into this book.

The responses to the online course were very positive last year and participants felt positive transformations from following the course.

You may be interested in my channeled Sacred White Flame Initaitons and Activations which I received in 2018 and was guided to share with others. Since initially attuning a few people to this beautiful energy I have created a distance learning initiation to this sacred energy in two parts: Sacred White Rose Initiation and Sacred White Flame Activation. There will soon be the third part of Teacher/Master White White Flame Attunements for others to teach this special energy frequency.

In the third part you will be initiated to the Order of the White Flame and ancient order of the Eygptian mysteries and learn how to attune others to this energy. It is the energy of "Now" it is ascension energy and it comes to us with from the energies of the Divine Council of Light, from Mary Magdalene and Yeshua and from Goddess Isis and her son Horus. It comes with a perfect balance of white light from Divine Femimine and Divine Masculine. For more information about the Sacred White Flame visit my website https://www.orarosetemple.com/white-flame-ascension

Currently I am creating a second meditation course called "Rainbow Rays for Ascension" this will be available soon with an ebook and eight meditations these include White Flame, Pink Bliss, Magenta Rays, Amethyst Flame and Diamond Light.

I am a keen photographer and the photographs in this book are my own photos. I also like to write poetry and you can find some of my poems on my website.

Kim Ora Rose at Sainte Baume, Mary
Magdalene Grotte 2019

Carasonne & Chatsworth House Water Cascade

Photographs by Kim Ora Rose

Kim Ora Rose

I have been a sensitive and a medium all my life, I have memories of seeing angels in my garden as a child and I was often woken up in the night by sounds and images. In my early childhood we lived in a new bungalow opposite a Norman church with links back into history. The church always fascinated me, I have always been drawn to the buildings, liked to wander around the pews, settle down for a quiet prayer and muse at the graves of those passed on to another realm.

In Stogursey a small village in the rural area of Somerset. The church of St Andrew dates back from early twelfth century and is now a Grade 1 listed building. It was previously a Benedictine priory church and before that a pagan site.   The church holds many secrets and ghosts that would frequent the grave yard and stream running by.

Later we moved to an old farm cottage on the edge of the Quantock hills and this was one of the most idyllic places we had known, surrounded by fields of wonder and magic.

As a young teenager I used to read playing cards and my mother would tell us about seeing spirits. This seemed the most natural thing to talk about, she had the gift of seeing loved ones after they had passed over she had the gift of clairvoyance. My early gifts came in the form of inner knowing, sensing spirit and my clairvoyance came later. After my mother died in 2000 I sought to understand life and death and especially the realms of the spirit in all it forms. I became a medium/channeller and communicate with the spirit world, angelic realms, ascended masters, goddesses/gods, divine feminine, Brotherhood of Light and the Divine Council of Light.

Healing was always at the core of my being I am a Magdalene Priestess, Intuitive Energy Healer, flower healer, Reiki Master Teacher (Usui & Karuna Ki), Founder of Sacred White Flame Heading Modality, Founder of Pink Bliss Healing Ray, Angelic Reiki Practitioner, Colour Therapy Practitioner, Herbalist, Crystal Healer and Soul to Soul Healing.

I have experienced several awakenings; after receiving my Reiki 11 attunement I went through a period of massive expansions, was guided by spirit guides, higher self and my healing guide of Lao Tzu. During this time I created a system of communicating with my spiritual guidance team and this strengthened my psychic and mediumship abilities. I used to journal with "Great Spirit" and with "God" this was very private to me which I didn't share with others.

Once I shared my system of identifying my spiritual team around with another medium and she said she had never known anything like it, this worried me so I closed down for a while. Now I know that there was nothing to worry about at all, there is nothing unusual about speaking directly with God, with Yeshua and Mary Magdalene in addition to my other spiritual team. I had another massive awakening in 2019 after my pilgrimage to France and celebrating Mary Magdalene's feast day in Glastonbury.

During this awakening I received another gift of light, this time from Jesus in the form of the purist love I had ever felt, it was so passionate and took me through a few weeks of transformation and healing. Jesus showed me how *love* was at the heart of everything and how to express this love more with everyone. I call this the *Passion of Christ* and it comes with the colour Red.

A couple of months ago the two energies of Mary Magdalene's Pink Bliss and Jesus's Passion of Christ were united to become a new energy source within me of a Cerise colour. When I receive these direct energy sources I always associate with a colour, this is my unique way of understanding them.

Colours are a core part of my communication with spirit and my guides so this is how I process new energies. Other people might do this in a completely different way and you too may identify energy that comes to you in a different way.

This is all perfect, however we receive energy, how we channel and receive is perfect for us, there is no need to compare with others as this can lead to separation.

Although I have lived a past life at the time of Mary Magdalene I first became interested in her about eight or nine years ago. I was guided to first read about her and was then guided to be a Magdalene Priestess this was a pinnacle part of my life. It was a time when I was guided each step of the way. I am a Magdalene High Priestess and teach others. I am a light bearer, wayshower and oracle I offer soul guidance, soul healing and spiritual teachings.

As a child I wanted to be a school teacher and started teaching in 2004 Business Studies and ICT in secondary schools until I retired from teaching in 2016.

One of my key messages and guidance from my life is to encourage everyone that anything is possible and to live your dreams.

I have a little rule about "no rules" this comes from years of rules and doubts that others impart on us about our own creativity, I have had teachers who give you rules, rules for how you do something for example rules for painting, use this paint, these brushes these techniques when in fact when you start from a place of experiment you can use what every you wish to use. I started painting with acrylics last year and use the similar formula no rules, so I could use watercolour, pastels, felt tips and create anything I liked. I have utilised this technique with my poems and prose, by taking out any expectations of creating with a format or pattern it leads to perfect creations.

So this is very much part of everything now, pure creativity and unlimited potentials with total freedom.

For several years I ran a series of psychic development courses, angel/ascended master meditation classes, reiki healing and spiritual mystic readings. I now offer Soul Readings and Soul Healing which is much deeper than psychic work it goes deeper below the obvious and into the inner working of the memory, mind and emotions where we hold our deepest secrets and memories.

Since a small child I've always been fascinated by "Tea"

and different types of tea with flowers, herbs, leaves, roots etc. I have recollections of making rose tea with rose petals from our childhood garden, making herb teas and tinctures. Countless memories of making fresh peppermint tea, sage tea and lavender tea. Tea is a quiet passion of mine which I am sure comes from another life as a herbalist. There is so much power in flowers, I studied the Bach Flower Healing system and am learning more about the healing properties of flowers. You may wish to drink different types of tea to correspond with each of the rose colours as you proceed through this program eg drink rose, lavender etc tea.

I have now published my Mystical Flower Guardians Series; Flowers of the Quantocks is about my childhood memories in Somerset, Flower Healing is the Spiritual Guidance from 29 flowers there is a deck of cards available from my website that can be used with this book, plus Gaia's Healing Garden.

This book is an international best selling and is available as an ebook, paperback and hardback. It will be available as an audio book format in December. This book holds the Pink Bliss energy at its heart, its full of information about how to use flowers for healing. There are 29 flowers in the book and lots of information about how to connect with seasons, elements, chakras, the Spirit Guardians, meditations and spiritual guidance. Plus a how to create your own flower essences, flower bowl healing, tea ceremonies etc section too.

We know that we can program crystals and we can program water too. It holds intention, holds memories and you can add your own intentions or spells to the water you drink for example I use water blessings on my drinks and create water bowls for healing.

I have a collection of crystal pendants that have been programmed to hold the energy with bio-resonance technology that you can wear to boost the keywords, energies of the flowers, and holds the vibrations of Mary Magdalene and Mother Mary. I have some for other flowers and their guardians that are part of my mystical flower guardian - Gaia's Healing Garden collection.

You can find these pendants on www.orarosetemple.com in the Temple Shop area.

Bioresonance is energy balancing and enhancing through quantum entanglement, clearing energetic blockages and interferences in your biofield. My friend Kerry Mitchell uses a eLybra device that was produced by World Development Systems, who have developed a range of other Bioresonance products including wearable pendants and water enhancer mats, available. She creates a whole range of products with her eLybra device.

If you come across a blockage on your spiritual journey she can run a program to clear your blockage and can create you a pendant, mat or other item to hold that energy for you. Just as these meditations in this book help you clear blockages and move forward, bio resonance can help you clear deep core issues eg childhood trauma, family issues, lack of self worth from childhood triggers etc.

You can visit Kerry's page to see more about bio resonance and her products, she is an artist too and uses programmed crystals in her artwork.

https://www.ascensionart.co.uk/

*O*ther courses available:

Usui Reiki 1, 11 & 111 Master Teacher

Magdalene Priestess Training

Magdalene High Priestess Training

Rainbow Rays Ascension Course

Sacred White Rose Initiation

Sacred White Flame Activation

Immaculate Heart of Mother Mary Reiki

Heart of Mary Magdalene Reiki

Mary Magdalene Pink Bliss Ray Attunement

Aphrodite Shining Star Reiki Attunement

Reiju Empowerment - Refresher

Munay Ki Nine Rite

13th Rite of the Womb

Goddess Isis Priestess Training launching soon....

To find out more about Kim Ora Rose visit her website www.orarosetemple.com

About The Author

Kim Ora Rose

Kim Ora Rose is a Magdalene Priestess, Medium, Healer and Spiritual Teacher she lives is a retired teacher and lives in the Midlands, United Kingdom with her family and two dogs. She is an author of self help books and a founder of White Flame Healing, Pink Bliss Ray and Blue Lotus Flower Reiki.

www.orarosetemple.com

Praise For Author

"What a wonderful book this is bringing the deeply mystical healing and awakening qualities of the white flame. There are so many mystical teachings shared here with beautiful healings included. Kim has provided ancient teachings brought into the modern day to assist you on your journey to the self and she shares many tools and inspiration throughout the book. Kim's deep connection to spirit shines through every word written and she is passionate about sharing it for the benefit of others. Journey with her through this book to the deepest aspects of the self and you will find healing for yourself and a deepening of your consciousness. "
Margaret Hunt

"Receiving the White Flame initiation from Kim was an amazing and powerful experience! It not only raised my vibration but also connected me to very high vibrational beings such as Isis, Mother Mary, and other members of what are termed the Council of Light."

-JRK

"Mary Magdalene sat holding my hand as I cried with

gratitude. It went black and she said "it is the secret knowledge we have put in Suzanne. We want you to speak out to your family, friends, sisters and anyone who will listen."

- SG

"I started the course a few days late however I completed all 22 days. The course was 7 meditations, each meditation was repeated 3 times over 21 days. I found the meditations to be very profound. I felt that each time I did the same meditation something would come up that needed to be released. I felt a lot of love in each meditation that helped me release my "stuff". I felt a deep sense of support & reassurance from the meditations. Kim is a lovely teacher. She has a lovely sense of humour & made me feel very relaxed. I do feel. there is a positive difference in me, following the programme. I feel lighter in myself & more at peace. Thank you Kim xxx

- ZEE

Thank you so much Kim for part one of the free abundance course you so kindly shared. During those 22 days I felt lots of cleansing was taking place from my phy body removing density from my bones and muscles that caused pain and aches, particularly in the hands. I remember you telling me a few months back I used to have power in my hands but I lost it, well I felt the trauma of this was being cleansed away by the power within those 8 meditations. As a result, I am able to connect more strongly with my spirit team and receive lots of creative inspiration to feel the resistances I once *experienced when implementing new ideas or when taking action on something. I feel doubt has been replaced with a willingness to just try with the feeling of excitement and curiosity in my heart. I am so grateful to you Kim for offering this as it has certainly made a very positive impact on my life so far."*

-J KEALL

"Mystical Flower Guardians is a book you will want to refer to again and again as it is packed with so much information regarding the magic, the mystery and the healing of the flowers. Reading through every page it is so apparent that Kim has such a deep love for nature and along with that love is a very profound wisdom of the healing properties which are to be found in each flower."

- MARGARET HUNT

Mystical Flower Guardian - Gaia's Healing Garden

Welcome to Mystical Flower Guardians, Gaia's Healing Garden to her flowers and trees to my collection of flower healers and their mystical flower guardians. Welcome to the realms of Plant Medicine the language of flowers and their incredible Guardians. Mystical flowers are full of light, they each have their own Spirit Guardian which holds the highest potential of healing light and guides us as we connect with them. Each flower holds its own vibration and light frequency and as you connect to each of them you will blend with their light. You will become to know each of the Mystical flowers as friends and will learn how how to connect deeply to their magical powers and mystical ways of being.

You shall go on a mystical, magical enchanted journey with Gaia's healing flowers; you may already work or know many of the flowers but through this book, you will explore hidden depths to explore the healing benefits of each of the flowers, how to use different parts of the flowers to use and you will meet the flower guardians through the meditation journeys to their sacred places. You will go deeper than ever before with each of the flowers. This is a remarkable journey, that you may have never gone on before. You may have been aware of flower fairies or elementals. In this book, you will go so much deeper to meet each of the Guardians and know their healing powers.

Prepare yourself to dive deep into the realms of flowers in Gaia's Healing Garden with flower essences, teas, essential oils and journey meditations.

Flowers Of The Quantocks

his book takes you through my early childhood with memories and snippets of history about the places I lived in, we moved houses several times in Somerset until we finally settled in the Midlands. We continued to visit our family for the summer holidays for many years and my heart is in those country villages and my love of wildflowers too.

It is a prequel to my Mystical Flower Guardians book that will be published in 2022 this is a book about healing with flowers and spirit guardians. Kim is a mystic, medium, healer, priestess, and channeller who has written a book about flower healing with meditations and a deep connection to each flower's unique spirit guardian.

Kim was born in Somerset and was forever linked to this beautiful county with its magic and mystery through relations.

Mystical Flower Guardians - Flower Healing

Mystical Flower Guardians is a book about flower healing with flowers it is a unique healing system of healing with flowers and their spirit guardians eg Lavender and Goddess Hera, Lily, and Goddess Isis. This book accompanies Kim Ora Rose's healing cards and was channeled directly through the flowers themselves and the Council of Light. The book is based on flowers with their guardians, seasons, elements, chakras, planets, and keywords for spiritual healing.

The flowers can be used for divination and there are card layouts in the book to use.

This mystical flower healing system is unique for healing the mind, body and spirit. You can use the flowers in many ways and as your intuition guides you.

Sacred Temple Of The White Flame

White Flame is a unique powerful healing modality that prepares you for ascension and higher personal development. This is a gift from Soul to Soul, it will open you up to unlimited energies from the Sacred Temple of the White Flame.

This unique healing modality was channelled by Kim Ora Rose in 2018 it was through her advanced dedication with Mary Magdalene that she received the White Flame energies and symbols. It is overseen by the Divine Council of Light, Goddess Isis and her son Horus. Through Kim's spiritual journey as a medium, mystic, and healer she channelled white light for healing and creating sacred space. After her advanced dedication to Mary Magdalene and her search for the truth, she connected with the Divine Council of Light. They are a collective consciousness of multi-dimensional light beings who are supporting the Earth's ascension. White Flame is a "Soul-to-Soul" gift, a healing modality that opens gateways to ancient wisdom from the Egyptian Temples of Isis and Horus. Learning about the ancient symbols and being initiated to the Sacred Temple of the White Flame.

The White Flame is for anyone who wishes to raise their vibrations on their spiritual journey to happiness, joy, contentment, health, abundance, and pure bliss. You can have these things in your life through daily healing, cleansing of old wounds and being open to limitless joy. It is for anyone who wishes to raise their vibrations on their journey to happiness, contentment, health, abundance and pure bliss.

Printed in Great Britain
by Amazon

86000570R00132